THEY PLAYED
THROUGH THE ECHO
OF THE WHISTLE

THEY PLAYED THROUGH THE ECHO OF THE WHISTLE

The story of how Valdosta State became a basketball dynasty

FRED GIBBONS

SWP
SpringfieldWoods Publishing
ST. AUGUSTINE, FL

SpringfieldWoods Publishing

Contents

Foreword: by Jackie Bradford

During my career as a high school and college basketball player, head basketball coach at Greater Atlanta Christian School, and former President and CEO of the Atlanta Tip-off Club and Naismith Awards, I competed against, observed, and worked alongside great players, teams, and coaches at the high school and collegiate levels throughout the country. I grew up in Lowndes County, Georgia, just up the road from Valdosta, Clyattville, and Dasher. Little did I know then that my professional life would be intertwined with coaches and players from those three South Georgia communities.

I played basketball at Pine Grove School. Just down the road in Valdosta was another 6-5 player, Jim Nichols. We competed throughout high school, using our baby hook shots and wrestling for rebounds. After graduation, Jim signed with Vanderbilt University and I signed with Freed-Hardeman College. We lost contact for a short time.

I returned home after one semester and went to work for the Owens-Illinois plant in my hometown and continued to play basketball in an Industrial League. Gary Colson, the new Head Coach at Valdosta State, played in the same league. Gary, was from Dasher, is six years older than me, so we never competed until the Industrial League. After working four years at Owens-Illinois, and the death of my father, I was determined to return to college and complete my education. Although Gary offered me a scholarship, I signed with Alabama Christian College, a first-year program, to play for Willard Tate. While we beat Auburn's freshman team twice my first year, the game against Colson's Valdosta State Rebels would provide an opportunity for me to renew my acquaintance with Jim Nichols, who I saw warming up for the Rebels. I later discovered he had been seriously injured at Vandy, and after coming home to recuperate, he walked on at Valdosta State. During his career with the Rebels, his passion, inside presence, and physicality showed no signs of the injury. Coach Colson had the young and improving Rebels headed toward a great year and they had their way with us that night in Valdosta.

Jim and I did not see each other for a number of years, as he served in the Vietnam War and then led a medical device company; whereas I went on to play basketball at David Lipscomb College under Charlie Morris, the same coach Gary Colson played for. Greater Atlanta Christian School was opening their doors and Jesse Long hired me as their Head Basketball Coach. I wore a number of hats while serving at GACS, one of which included participating and leading community related activities like the Atlanta Tip-Off Club. Garland Pinholster, who was from Clyattville, was the legendary Oglethorpe College Head Basketball Coach and preceded me as the President of the Atlanta Tip Off Club and the Naismith Awards. The relationship I developed with the now-deceased Pinholster, was special for a number of reasons. He grew up just down the road from me in South Georgia, was a role model, mentor, an inspirational leader, and one of the toughest competitors ever to roam a sideline in Georgia.

One of the Atlanta Tip-Off Club's objectives was to continue to elevate and enhance the profile of college basketball in Georgia. We chose to recognize the winningest coaches in Georgia, which included former GIAC foes Gary Colson (who was at the University of New Mexico) and Bill Foster (who was at Clemson). Although I had followed Gary's successful career, we were no more than acquaintances at this point. Gary invited a group of former Rebels (including Bobby Ritch, Ray McCully, Jim Nichols, et al) to the event; and it was there that Jim and I renewed our acquaintance. During the events, Coach Pinholster, Coach Colson, Jim, and I reminisced about the rivalry between Oglethorpe and Valdosta State. All four of us grew up playing basketball in Lowndes County—what are the chances? I have often thought how ironic it is that three of us (Coach Pinholster, Coach Colson, and I) were inducted into either the Atlanta Sports Hall of Fame or the Georgia Sports Hall of Fame.

Coach Pinholster is considered to be one of the pioneers of collegiate championship basketball in Georgia, taking Oglethorpe College from meager beginnings to deep into the DII playoffs in the early '60s. Coach Colson's Valdosta State Rebels were a young and upcoming team at that time, at the height of Oglethorpe's success. During our conversations at the event in Atlanta, Coach Pinholster had a poignant memory about the Rebels. He shared that Gary Colson took his "Wheel Offense" and adapted it to the point the Rebels eventually swept the season series by the mid-60s, a changing of the guard in the upper echelon of college basketball in Georgia. Coach Pinholster jokingly said Colson drove him out of basketball. The truth was Coach Pinholster was given much more executive and administrative responsibility within Oglethorpe College's executive leadership team, and therefore retired from coaching. From that point on, Jim, Coach Pinholster, Coach Colson, and I became close friends for life.

Recently, Jim called on behalf of the Rebel Legacy Project Team to ask If I would read this book (and write a Foreword) that captures this magical era of Valdosta State basketball from 1954-1972. I agreed and am thankful I had the chance to read this inspiring tale of teams that played "through the echo of the whistle" and won 11 GIAC Championships in 12 years. As a former head coach, I was intrigued by their ability to dominate their competition consistently, under three different head coaches within those 12 years. This book's fascinating perspective piqued my interest, and I soon discovered the Valdosta State Rebels were not only successful but were a dynasty in that era; and the writer provides insights into the reasons they were successful year after year.

The further I read, the more amazed I became with the stories and insights into the coaches, players, and each season, as the book traced the development of the program from a club team to perennial conference champions. Having competed against Valdosta State in the early years of this dynasty, the book ignited memories long ago shelved away in my mind of the rabid nature of the fans in Valdosta, and the amount of noise they created! I vividly remembered the level of extraordinary intensity with which those teams played the game from beginning to end. The book's title, *They Played Through the Echo of the Whistle*, reminded me of what it was like playing against the likes of Jim Nichols and Chuck Bonovitch under the backboards! As the pages unfurled, the stories of the players were informative in that character mattered as much or more than talent to the head coaches. The coaches had a name for that character, the Rebel Spirit, which contributed to their sustained success as a team.

This inspiring story tells how players with character and talent were transformed by the head coaches who knew how to create a championship culture that shows the effects of great leadership from beginning to end! All of these men, Valdosta State coaches, staff, and players were united in their commitment to pursue perfection and experience excellence!

– Jackie

Dedication

This book is dedicated to the men who played, coached, and served on the staff of the Valdosta State College basketball program during the years 1954-1972, AKA, the "Rebels." To these men, becoming a "Rebel" was a privilege and honor earned, not an entitlement.

Especially, it is dedicated to our brothers, our teammates who have passed on from this world. Each of you meant the world to us! So many times, we think back to a moment, a play, and things we talked about and smile; for example, when Bill Summerford said with a straight face, "always a bridesmaid, never a bride" describing Shorter's futile efforts to unseat the Rebels. We gathered the memories of those glorious and happy (as well as heartbreaking) moments in this book to ensure our efforts and accomplishments were not in vain and forgotten but will be shared with the generations of families within our brotherhood. Following is a list of known teammates including the years they played. (This list is the information available at the time of printing)

Bob Anderson (1960-61)

Robert Bailey (1961-62)

Chuck Bonovitch (1962-64)

Homer Chambliss (1960-61)

Syrup Deariso (1965-68)

Eric Mance (1970-74)

John McIntyre (1958-60)

Robert McKinney (1967-68)

Gene Peacock (1958-59)

Letson Plant (1964-66)

Bill Strong (1963-64)
Wayne Studdard (1958-59)
Bill Summerford (1962-64)
John Trimnell (1966-70)
Willie Yarborough (1969-1973)

Lastly, it is dedicated to providing our children, grandchildren, and great grandchildren with a glimpse of this unmatched era of college basketball at a small, public university in South Georgia that went from a start-up outfit in 1954 to become a perennial conference champion, a dynasty within the GIAC, and a national championship contender during the 60s and early 70s.

Prologue

"The Thoughts of Youth are Long, Long Thoughts!"

One of Henry Wadsworth Longfellow's great lines of poetry is "A boy's will is the wind's will, And the thoughts of youth are long, long thoughts." This refrain hears Longfellow reflecting back with fond memories of his hometown as a boy, and while the boy in him may be lost in time, the memories exist vividly in the hallways of his mind. In this one short line of poetry, Longfellow captures the heart and minds of all who walk down the path of aging, not so much looking to the future but looking back over a long life lived, which went all too quickly it seems.

For a number of years, there has been a discussion and some action regarding capturing the history and legacies of the opening chapter of Valdosta State Basketball, 1954-1972. Many coaches, players, and staff from that era retain close relationships and are in constant contact with one another. In February 2020, former Head Coach Gary Colson (1958-1968), was inducted into the Georgia Sports Hall of Fame in Macon. The Induction Ceremony was attended by over 75 former players, staff, and families, which says something of the endearing relationships between the head coach, his staff, and players. While in Macon, the former coaches, players, and staff discussed the status of the Rebel Legacy Project and what needed to be done to bring it to fruition and conclusion. A commitment was made by a core group, the Rebel Legacy Project Team, to facilitate and finish the project. The original members of the Rebel Project Team were: Ray McCully, Mike Perry, Bobby Ritch, Tommy Johnson, Jim Nichols, and Fred Gibbons. The three head coaches were also included in discussions: Gary Colson, Jim Melvin, and James Dominey.

Since then, the Project Team has contacted former players, asking for their feedback and memories regarding what brought them to Valdosta State, the key games and players, and what the impact of the experience of being a part of the Rebel brotherhood was on their life afterward. This book would not have been possible without the contributions of the Project Team, former players, and staff who have responded. Thank you for the thoughtful and touching memories you shared. You helped to preserve for all time the historical tapestry of that era of Valdosta State Basketball, a half century ago.

Just as Longfellow said, "the thoughts of youth are long, long thoughts," the former coaches, staff, and players from that era began to reflect back through the corridors of time to the relationships within the locker room and on the floor, to the victories and championships, to meeting our respective spouses in many cases, and being student athletes and obtaining our degrees. Over 30 alumni responded, and the consensus is that the overall experience of being a Rebel is practically indescribable; a once-in-a-lifetime experience that has continued on because of the relationships extended throughout our lives! While there is no doubt we never experience the "powerful eau de cologne of the locker room" or the sting of heart-stopping losses or the thrill of victories as much as we did in those years; the memories are burnt into our minds, as indelible in our hearts and minds as Longfellow's memories were to him! You never forget those moments!

Upon arriving home in March, we began the journey to recover and explore the history of the Rebels through the "shifting nature" of our foggy memories, to ascertain the gravity and legacy of what we accomplished as a team year after year. We concluded that we needed some structure for this archaeological dig into our memories. We made use of recognized external and professional resources to assist in this historical journey, a complete list of which is in the Bibliography.

As we journeyed through the tunnel of time into the recesses of our minds, yearbooks, faded newspaper articles, and interviews, we asked three questions:

- How special were the Rebels during the era under review? Is there an external standard that can be applied to assist in defining "special?"
- The Rebels won lots of games and conference championships. Why? How did they have sustained success year after year?
- Why have teammates remained close all of these years?

The remainder of the Prologue provides you with the insights regarding how to determine how successful the Rebels were, whether or not they were a dynasty, as well as how those elite teams are developed and maintained over a decade. The professionals are from a variety of disciplines: an ESPN analyst, a Wall Street Journal writer, distinguished and recognized Leadership and Organizational Development leaders and writers, former college basketball players, and college and pro coaches. The Prologue is designed to provide some structure as you unfurl the pages and "forage through the thickets and clearings" of the history of these legendary Rebel Basketball squads. We believe it will become evident why these teams won championships and what the legacies of these Champions are!

The Mark of a Dynasty: "Can you do it for a decade?"

Sam Walker (noted columnist from the WSJ) answers the question, "how special were these Rebels," in his book *The Captain Class*. Walker's research points out that for a team to be considered a dynasty, they must exhibit "sustained domination over their peers." Walker uses professional franchises like the 60s Celtics, which won 10 championship rings in 11 years, as examples. Tiger Woods provides more clarity on what constitutes a dynasty by pointing out that "it all comes down to how long a team can dominate their league; can you do it for a decade?"

The Rebels' numbers between 1958 - 1972 answer the question rather convincingly: The Rebels went 246-113 (68%) during the regular season and 138-30 (82%) within the GIAC, winning the GIAC Championship 11 out of 12 years between 1960-1972. In addition, the Rebels played in 11 NAIA District 25 Tournaments, winning three times to earn the coveted trip to the NAIA National Championship in Kansas City (the only team from that decade and district to win the District 25 title three years in a row). Although the Rebels are not NBA Champions, they did dominate their peers (GIAC) convincingly for 12 years. In that context and era, they were an elite dynasty according to Walker and Woods!

How did the Rebels develop and sustain a championship culture over 12 years?

Walker ruled out things like raw talent, tactics, and money. His research indicated that the influence and power of both Bench (coaches and staff) and Floor (players) Leadership are the two most critical ingredients in not only creating an elite championship culture, but more importantly empowering and equipping the elite teams to "win championships for a decade or more."

Key Element #1: Bench Leadership

Seth Davis, renowned ESPN Basketball analyst and writer, penned *Getting to Us* to examine college coaches with sustained success over decades in the hope of figuring out how they get to "us." Davis notes that teams begin with a collection of Jimmy's and Joe's, and it is the head coach's job to figure out a way to get them from "me to us."

"A team's cultural resonance and the size of its trophy cabinet don't play positions on the field. A team's ability to uphold a tradition of excellence comes down to something rather mundane – the quality of its upper management." Sam Walker

---

He refers to this alchemy as a "mysterious process by which the coach is able to stir his players to reach their potential as individuals and as a unit" as the signature of elite Bench Leadership.

Walker's and Davis' works offer substantive research and years of observation, and while credible, it is somewhat subjective. What Davis refers to as a **"mysterious process"** employed by successful Bench Leadership (coaches) to unlock the potential of their teams is an exhibition of what leadership experts refer to as Transformational Leadership. Following are the behaviors and core values Transformational Leaders exhibit—the keys to the kingdom of sustained success for any executive leader or head coach:

- Model of integrity and fairness. Authentic. They "walk the talk."
- Humble, able, and willing to set aside ego and assumptions. Self-aware, a lifelong learner who is always moving toward Personal Mastery.
- Disciplined, determined, persistent, resilient, and committed to hard work.
- Sets clear goals.
- Has high expectations.

- Excels at relationship management. Demonstrates respect, empathy, actively listens and provides constructive feedback.
- Encourages others. Provides support and recognition. Stirs the emotions of people.
- Gets people to look beyond their self-interest; effectively creates a Shared Vision.
- Inspires people to reach for the improbable, reach beyond "what is" for "what can be."
- Team builder, develops team feedback loops, defines clear team roles, and provides team learning opportunities.

As you read the following pages, refer back to this list to discover the qualities of each of the architects of the Rebels' success. There were four head coaches of the Rebels during this period, yet all were Transformational in some form and manner. The book is broken down into four sections, one for each of the head coaches. There, you will discover their leadership, management, coaching styles, and skills. You will hear from players and staff regarding what made them successful and effective.

Key Element #2: Floor Leadership (Captains and others)

"The single most important ingredient after you get the talent is internal leadership. It's not the coaches as much as one single person or people on the team who set higher standards than that team would normally set for itself."
Duke Basketball Coach Mike Krzyzewski

Next, Walker and Davis point out that that Bench Leadership does not mean much once the ball is tipped and the game begins. That is why Walker says, "The most crucial ingredient in a team that achieves and sustains historic greatness is the character of the player(s) who lead it."

He pointed out that Floor Leaders (players) have eight distinct traits, they are:

- Rarely the stars.
- Extremely competitive, doggedly determined —relentless and resilient.
- The epitome of a Servant Leader: Humble, willing to do the thankless jobs in the shadows on both the floor and in the locker room.
- Exceptionally low key, practical, and effective communicators who have the respect of everyone and were the moral authority for the team.
- Aggressive players that test the limits of the rules, "play through the echo of the whistle."
- Constantly motivating others with their passionate and extraordinary non-verbal actions and plays during competition and practice.
- Courageous, willing to hold firm to their strong convictions, to stand apart, and if necessary, stand up for what they believed in.
- Able to maintain ironclad emotional control in competition.

The Floor Leadership (captains and other players) are the glue and the driving force, the sparkplug, the motivator, and the disciplinarian within the locker room and on the floor that propels teams to remain great over sustained periods of time. As explore this brief history, you will run across stories of players and teams who played with palpable passion and purpose. In our mind's eye, we can see them (and the rest of the Rebels) play at levels that amazed their fans and tormented their opponents. They played and conducted themselves with an uncommon spirit, what is referred to as the Rebel Spirit!

The Architects of the Rebels' Success, the head coaches, clearly knew how to select not only talented players, but more importantly, young men with great character. Young men who were willing to be coached, embraced teamwork and hard work, and were most of all, extremely aggressive and tough (resilient and relentless). These Architects of Success effectively used the mysterious process of team building to mold these Jimmy's and Joe's into Us, the Valdosta State Rebels....along the way teaching us to "play through the echo of the whistle" leading to the gold standard in athletics: 11 GIAC Championships in 12 years! A dynasty unlike any other in the history of college basketball in Georgia!

I

Introduction

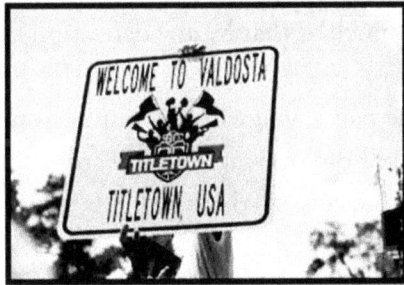

In 1977 Mike Chason, the young Sports Editor of the Valdosta Daily Times, referred to Valdosta, Georgia as "Winnersville." Years later, Valdosta was labeled as "Titletown" by news agencies such as Sports Illustrated, ESPN, and the New York Times. Both titles were connected to the vaunted Valdosta Wildcats football dynasty, led by legendary coaches Wright Bazemore and Nick Hyder for much of the last half of the 20th century. Although the Wildcats have won more games than any high school in history, they now share the "Titletown" moniker with Lowndes HS and Valdosta State football teams, both of whom have won championships in the last 25 years. Visiting Valdosta is characterized as a trip to a stadium or gym where visiting teams' dreams come to die.

Valdosta is a rabid, championship-hungry community where winning was and still is part of the fabric of the community. Residents insist on not just winning games, but winning championships. Football season winds down by Christmas at the high school level, as well as FBS Division II. Into this lull after football season stepped Rebel basketball in 1954.

The purpose of this book is to focus on the accomplishments, qualities, and characteristics of the Rebel basketball culture within the 1954-72 era, the effect that experience had on the lives of the men who were Rebels, and the legacy of the teams to the university, community, and their respective families and careers. These were the formative years of the Valdosta State basketball program, where a championship culture was developed and nurtured by the respective coaches. Between 1960-1972, Rebel basketball became a sustained high performing team-oriented culture, so much so that by any definition they were a dynasty within the GIAC.

As you read these pages, you will find out what made this team and era so special. You will discover: 1) who the architects of success were, and their secrets to success; 2) the highlights of the most significant games of each season, including the special moments and memories for each season, from the perspective of the players, staff, and fans; and 3) the makeup of the indomitable Rebel Spirit that enabled the Rebels to play through the echo of the whistle, propelling each team to perform at a championship level, year in and year out.

The Records from Year to Year

Just how special was the first chapter of Valdosta State Basketball? Compare and consider that UCLA (under the legendary John Wooden) won 82% of their conference games during his career. Valdosta State also won 82% of their conference games during this era. Anytime a college has this degree of success, it is usually referred to as a dynasty. For the other GIAC members, it was more like a nightmare that played on and on through 1972.

Although the following chart is a simple spreadsheet, it reveals what the patterns and trends were during this era of basketball. This book will help you discover how this level of success occurred under the different coaches. In addition, you will learn what the common threads are that connect these teams over the era, although the personnel often changed from one year to the next.

Year	Won	Lost	Pct.	Conf.	Won	Lost	Pct.	Finish
1954-55	2	3	40	-	-	-	-	-
1955-56	2	8	20	-	-	-	-	-
1955-56	2	13	13.3	-	-	-	-	-
1957-58	3	11	21.4	-	-	-	-	-
1958-59	11	9	55	GIAC	8	6	57.1	3rd
1959-60	9	15	37.5	GIAC	6	8	42.9	5th
1960-61	18	6	75	GIAC	12	0	100	1st
1961-62	19	2	90.5	GIAC	12	0	100	1st
1962-63	14	8	63.6	GIAC	8	2	80	1st
1963-64	15	6	71.4	GIAC	7	3	70	1st
1964-65	16	4	80	GIAC	9	1	90	2nd
1965-66	24	5	82.8	GIAC	9	1	90	1st
1966-67	27	8	77.1	GIAC	11	1	91.63	1st
1967-68	23	10	69.7	GIAC	11	1	91.63	1st
1968-69	18	11	2	GIAC	14	0	100	1st
1969-70	19	11	63	GIAC	12	2	85.7	1st
1970-71	15	10	60	GIAC	9	3	75	1st
1971-72	18	8	39.2	GIAC	10	2	83.3	1st
Totals	255	148	63.2		138	30	82.1	

2

⚜

The Cottingham Years:
Laying the Cornerstone for
a Championship Dynasty

Introduction

Valdosta State University took a circuitous route to get to where it is today, a student body of more than 12,000 students, with five Colleges offering 56 undergraduate degree programs and over 40 graduate programs and degrees.

Originally, the school that would become Valdosta State University was founded in 1906. Colonel W.S. West led the legislation through the Georgia Senate, then C.R. Ashley and E.J. McRee pushed it through the House. However, no funds were appropriated for it until 1911, when the state allocated $25,000. The city of Valdosta raised $50,000, and Col. West gave the property that is now the main part of campus to the state for use by the new institution. The president chosen was Richard Holmes Powell. His travels in the American Southwest led him to choose the Spanish Mission style of architecture for the institution's buildings. The school opened as South Georgia State Normal College (SGSNC) in January 1913, with three college freshmen and 15 sub-freshmen. The early students were required to wear a school uniform and paid $10 per year for tuition and $12 per month for food and board. Most came to be teachers and studied subjects from literature to physics to agriculture. In 1922, the school became a four-year college and the legislature changed the name to Georgia State Women's College, which remained in place until 1950.

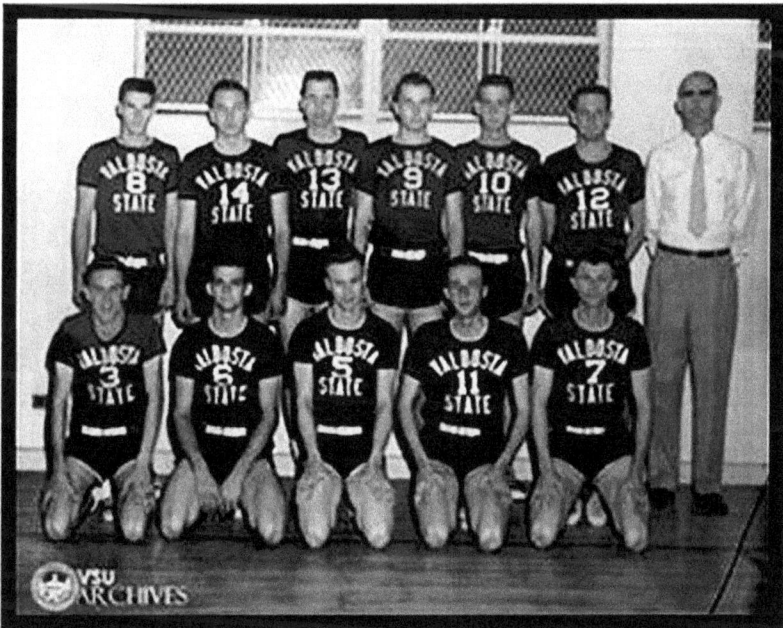

Walter Cottingham's first Valdosta Squad Front Row, left to right: Robert McElvey, Ray Cowart, Charles Casey, Buck Pafford, Ken Boyer Back Row: Gene Gray, Bill Long, Barney Purvis, Jesse Long, Roy McQuaid, Jimmy Stovall, Head Coach Walter Cottingham.

After WW II concluded, with GI's returning and the United States moving toward a "new normal" there was an emphasis on education, i.e., the GI Bill. Dr. Ralph Thaxton, who served at the University of Georgia, where he held roles as professor, Dean, Director of Admissions, and Registrar, became the third President of the College. Soon after Dr.

Thaxton began his service, the Board of Regents, acting on the advice of a committee which had examined the entire University of Georgia System, declared that in 1950 GSWC was to become co-educational—Valdosta State College (VSC). Under Dr. Thaxton's leadership, programs in pre-medical, pre-dentistry, and pre-pharmacy were added, the sciences became more prominent, and majors in Business Management became popular.

By 1956, the number of men on campus outnumbered the women, Greek organizations were formed, with fraternities leading the way, and intercollegiate athletics became a part of campus life when the Rebels, an all-male basketball team, was formed in 1954.

Dr. Thaxton, VSC'c President as Interscholastic sports began.

Dr. Thaxton tapped Walter Cottingham as the Head Coach and Athletic Director. The Rebel basketball program was born with little fanfare and even less money. The talent on hand consisted of club basketball players and there was no gym. Cottingham was the right man for this start-up project. If you know anything about start-up projects, it usually takes from three to five years to get them off the ground, and nothing is guaranteed other than as a leader you had better be flexible, able, and willing to adapt to overcome both known and unknown challenges (opportunities) that fall in your path when the headwinds grow fierce.

Here are four observations about Coach Cottingham;

- He was courageous. Otherwise, he would not take on the mountain of a task like starting a collegiate athletic program from scratch, with no money, facility, or players.
- He was a dedicated and hard worker, who worked second jobs—officiating high school basketball games in the area. It was

in this role he came to become acquainted with Gary Colson, star player for Georgia Christian School out of Dasher. Colson and his mates won the State Championship before Colson left for David Lipscomb College. Coach Cottingham could not offer Colson a scholarship—he had no money—but he did envision Colson's leadership potential as the coach at Valdosta State. He told Colson before he left for Lipscomb, "get your Master's degree and come back here, because I have job for you."

• He was able to build a foundation. He and Dr. Thaxton were able to get the necessary funds for a gym and it was in place early in the program.

• He was humble. His ego never got in the way of his objective—get the program started, keep it up and running. He was a competitor but understood his role and was comfortable with it.

Jimmy Stovall

Bill Long (1954-55) offers this description:: "Coach Cottingham drove the bus on away games and would play live music on the radio. When 'Rock around the clock' came on, he would replace the last 'rock' with 'Rebels.' Coach never lost his cool, he was always a gentleman. He did not hesitate to ask us for advice on how to play at timeouts. He was willing to have in-depth conversations about life. He and I would talk religion sometimes. I learned from him. He was a highly active member of Park Avenue Methodist. He kept us in-line but was never hardnose. We all respected him. I never heard one player criticize him."

Barney Purvis, lead scoring two years in a row.

Cottingham's first squad, 1954-55, had 11 players and was captained by Bill Long. Budget constraints were tight, which affected scheduling. Long recollects they also played a number of military teams and junior colleges, finishing with a 12-14 record.

The leading scorers were Bill Long with 18.4 ppg and Barney Purvis with 16.8 ppg. Bill's brother, Jesse, and Gene Gray were contributors on this team. Bill believes the biggest win was versus Piedmont, "I had 20 or 25 points but the best was in the last 5 seconds with score tied, Gray got the ball, hit me at mid-court, I just let it fly and it went in! We won! The fans were screaming, including Dr. Thaxton! A great memory!"

Cottingham's second Rebels squad had some turnover from the first year, but Purvis was back along with Buck Pafford and Gray.

The Rebels would go 2-8 during the 1955-56 season but began to create interest and enthusiasm among the student body and the community. Although the crowds had not yet reached the full throated fanaticism that would be heard in the years to come, the seeds were placed in the hearts of the students and community!

The third year of Rebel Basketball (1956-57) proved to be another uphill climb for the young program, although there were some bright lights on the horizon.

Standing: Mike Newman, Jimmy Stovall, Al Stephens, Gene Cargile, Douglas Parrish, Ben Wood, Coach Cottingham. Kneeling: Johnny Pervis, Louie Shipes, Ed Gandy, O. W. Hodge and James David.

The Rebels went 2-13, but played 15 games, which is 50% more than the second year and 200% more than the first year. Money continued to be an issue for the fledgling program.

There were key players from this squad that would suit up in 1957-58: Jerry Studdard, Doug Parrish, Al Stevens, and Johnny Purvis. All four averaged double digits in the '57-'58 season, with Studdard averaging 23.3 ppg and Stevens averaging 12.9 ppg. With the program started, Cottingham's primary objective was to locate a new head coach.

Walter Cottingham's Accomplishments and Legacies

As the 1957-58 season concluded, the decision was made to search for a new basketball coach. Coach Cottingham, as the Athletic Director, assumed responsibility for this project, although he had already made a preliminary inquiry to Gary Colson five years ago.

Earlier, we mentioned Walter Cottingham often worked multiple jobs. While officiating high school games, he consequently came across a young man with extraordinary leadership potential. In effect, Cottingham's vision of the Head Coach of the Valdosta State Rebels was Gary Colson, who was completing his Master's degree in Nashville. Before we turn our attention to the Gary Colson era, following are Walter Cottingham's accomplishments.

Cottingham had been assigned the unenviable task of starting a program from scratch in an era of austere funding. Consequently, he literally had no scholarship funding, not much equipment to speak of, nor support staff, nor transportation. What he accomplished in his four years was remarkable considering the hurdles set in front of him.

Coach Cottingham literally and figuratively laid the initial cornerstone in place for Valdosta State Basketball. The Collins Dictionary defines a cornerstone as "the first stone set in the construction of a masonry foundation." This is the case with the Rebel Basketball culture. Furthermore, "all other stones will be set in reference to this stone, thus determining the position of the entire structure."

What were these cornerstones?

1. He brought Gary Colson on board as the second Head Basketball Coach in VSC history.
2. He recruited players who manifested the Rebel Spirit.
3. He oversaw the construction of the gym, the home of Rebel basketball for 18 years. It was the vaunted Death Valley of basketball,

where opponents' dreams came to die! It was hazardous to and loathed by opponents.

Another observation from Bill Long was that Coach Cottingham did an "incredible job laying the foundation for Gary to build on." Cottingham exemplified the servant leadership spirit in that he never let his ego get in the way of his task of providing a solid footing for the next head coach, which he knew was Gary Colson. In the spring of 1958, Walter Cottingham handed the baton off to a young (23 years old), fresh out of grad school coach. And as they say, the rest is history!

Coach Cottingham tosses the ball during practice.

3

The Colson Years: Catalyst
to a Championship Dynasty

As the 1957-58 season ended, Coach Cottingham zeroed in on hiring Gary Colson as the next Head Basketball Coach at Valdosta State.

As we all know, life is made up of natural talent hopefully mixed with the right people at the right time, shaken and stirred by life's experiences (some good, others not so good); all which leads to some degree of success in life, personally and professionally. Timing is everything, right? Gary refers to this as "fate", whereas others might say there is a lot of syn-

Coach Gary Colson

chronicity in Colson's life and career. Simply put, whether you use fate or synchronicity, one knows they are headed in the right direction when life winks and nods at you through events that appear to be unconnected at the moment but under further review sends this message that "you're headed down the best path for your life!" Cottingham seeing Colson in high school, acknowledging the potential leader in him and offering him the job is too much to be a coincidence!

Gary Colson was born to build championship cultures and coach! His passion and competitive spirit are just the beginning of his many attributes, talents, and gifts. And when we say "build championship cultures" what we mean is that Colson knows how to start from scratch and take the program to the next level, then the next level, etc. Wherever Gary Colson has gone as head coach, he left the program better than he found it. He is adept at practicing what the words of the song "Hey Jude" say: "Take a sad song and make it better." Whether at Valdosta State, Pepperdine University, New Mexico, or Fresno State, he left each one better.

Gary has an electric personality, is always energetic, personable, and positive, driven to win and has an uncanny ability and willingness to adapt and adjust based on the talent on his team in any given year. Colson's relationships with former players and coaches, as well as opposing and other coaches in the game of basketball, tend to be long term and positive. Consequently, his basketball network today stretches the breadth and scope of the game, from high school officials to NBA coaches and general managers throughout the college and international coaching ranks.

While at Lipscomb, Gary roomed with Jerry Jones, a player from Indiana, and their friendship became pivotal in Colson's coaching career. Jones and Colson have vastly different personalities, therefore they approached strategy, practice tactics, etc., differently; but they agreed on three things necessary to succeed at the college level: "recruiting, recruiting, and recruiting."

Recruiting was on the front of Coach Colson's mind once he arrived at VSC, because he knew as most coaches do that talent covers up a lot of coaching gaps. You can be the greatest coach in the world, but you better have some talent, or you are not going to win many games. His genuine and personable nature endeared him to coaches throughout the country, which created a rich and deep recruiting network.

Coach Colson knew he needed talent, so his first stop was his old roommate, Jerry Jones, who was coaching in Indiana. Gary called and inquired about finding ball players. Both coaches had an eye for talent (even if it was "potential" talent) and players with the character that would be necessary to get a foundation built around teamwork and collaboration. It was not long before the Indiana thoroughfare began to produce fruits from their labor: Ron Fortner, Bob Lamphier, John Trimnell, Marty Lehmann, and Mike Terry are just a few of the players produced by the close camaraderie of Colson and Jones.

At the same time Gary was laying a foundation at VSC, Benny Dees was doing the same thing in Tifton, GA at Abraham Baldwin Agricultural College (ABAC). As Gary tells the story, the next thing you know he and Dees would travel to the Indiana and Illinois high school championship games to scout and recruit. The relationship would last the length of both their college coaching careers. ABAC produced Rebels like Gwendell McSwain, his brother Carlos, Jimmy Dorsett, and others.

Although recruiting was critical, developing a system that put his players in the best position to win was just as critical. Colson's humility shows up at this point in his coaching journey as his coaching network was about to expand with regard to systems and structures within college basketball. Upon arriving at VSC, Coach Colson found Oglethorpe College was a yearly resident on the schedule (two games).

The Stormy Petrels were a stout opponent and successful at winning championships under the leadership of legendary coach, Garland Pinholster.

Colson's Relationships and Recruiting:

Someone once said, "I would rather be lucky than good." I have always considered myself lucky. I loved basketball, it loved me back. I was lucky to play in an era that was known as "The Golden Age of Indiana High School Basketball." I was lucky to play in a county that had 20 schools; in suburban Chicago that produced dozens of college players every year. I was lucky enough to be exposed to blacktop basketball on the "Courts" from grade school on. I was lucky enough to play on the best team, with the best player my school had produced. I was lucky enough to be on a sectional championship team, the "holy grail" of Indiana High School Basketball. Most of all, I was lucky enough to live in a town with Indiana's biggest gun shop!

The owner of the gun shop, Dick, employed a friend named Joe. Joe loved two things: guns and basketball. Joe had a twin brother who lived in Valdosta who also loved basketball and was acquainted with Gary Colson. In previous years, Joe had passed the word about a treasure trove of potential college players in a small accessible area to his brother in Valdosta, who told Colson. Coach Colson took advantage of this in a big way. The '66 team, that was nationally ranked and went to the Big Dance in Kansas City, had three starters from my county, plus four more players from Indiana. I was lucky enough to be "Colson's Last Rebel."

All of this luck and more lead to me being dropped in front of Barrow Hall on the North Campus of VSC with two suitcases and a cardboard box in the fall of 1967.

Marty Lehmann, Co-Captain 1970-71; Colson's last recruit from Indiana.

Colson shared in a recent conversation that after the first trip to Atlanta to play Oglethorpe, he wasn't sure what needed to be done, since Pinholster's outfit played a 1-3-1 zone that limited the Rebels to tough shots and not many rebounds, whereas on the other end, they proceeded to get and make layup after layup. The solution was to call on a friend and teammate from high school who lived in Atlanta (and played for Coach Cottingham at VSC), Bill Long ('54). Coach Colson said he asked Bill, who then enlisted his brother, Jesse, to scout the Petrels and send him the report identifying what they were doing defensively and offensively. Long went the extra mile, sending Colson an 8mm home movie of the entire game. Armed with a heavy amount of humility and an enduring competitive spirit, the determined Colson spent the better part of the next week breaking down Pinholster's vaunted offensive system, the "Wheel." Not only did he break it down, but he also installed it because it fit the team talent and culture he was developing—it was a team-oriented motion offense that required continuity of all five players. It is said "Imitation is the sincerest form of flattery." Coach Colson was humble, determined, and aware enough to see what was needed to be successful and made it happen. Adapt, adjust, and overcome! Creative problem solving was a huge gift in Colson's coaching tool belt.

4

1958-60: The Prelude to a Championship Dynasty

When Gary Colson arrived, he met with Dr. Thaxton and Shealy McCoy, comptroller for Valdosta State. During the meeting, a couple of items on the agenda were responsibilities, budget, and recruiting guidelines. Colson would be teaching PE classes, coaching the Cross Country and Tennis teams as well as Basketball. There would be limited funds available (and Colson would have to go through McCoy to get them), and they explained what was expected from him recruiting-wise. McCoy was known throughout the campus as a "tightwad with an attitude." He was a former Marine who seemed to enjoy intimidating anyone who came through his door asking for money. To this day, Colson gets queasy just talking about the face-to-face conversations he had with McCoy. While Dr. Thaxton was a fan and advocate for the basketball program, he allowed McCoy to run the operation of the school as he saw fit.

With the administrative meetings out of the way, the young head coach began assessing what resources he had in equipment, facilities, and players. "I went into the equipment room and there were old rubber PE basketballs, a few uniforms, and not much else," Colson says. "The gym was first class at that point. We basically had Chamber of Commerce scholarships ($30 a player) and no transportation to speak of." Nonetheless, the ever optimistic, competitive, and energetic Colson went about his passion: establishing a championship culture.

Front Row, Left to Right: Jan Rogers, John Moye, Hansel Faulkner, Wayne Garrick, John McIntyre, W. Studdard, Jerry Studdard Back row: Gene Holl (Mgr.) Head Coach Gary Colson, Gene Peacock, Buck Ethridge, Doug Parrish, Al Stevens, Pat Tomlinson, Hal Worley (Mgr.)

1958-59 Rebels, Colson's first Rebel team

Talent-wise, Colson believed he had three key lettermen returning: Doug Parrish, Al Stevens, and Jerry Studdard. All three players averaged double figures in their careers. In fact, Studdard averaged close to 23 ppg in his career and scored 729 points in his two years as a Rebel.

Although these three players were exceptionally good, Colson needed to locate and secure more talent if the Rebels were going to compete in the GIAC, as well as with Oglethorpe and Georgia Southern. New talent arrived in the form of Hansel Faulkner, Buck Ethridge, Gene Peacock, W. Studdard, Jimmy Stovall, Jan Rogers, John Moye, Wayne Garrick, John McIntyre, and Pat Tomlinson. Gary Colson's first campaign at Valdosta State got off to a positive start. Colson's energy and enthusiasm proved to be infectious and was reflected in the Rebels' play. The Rebels finished the season 11-9 overall and 8-6 in the GIAC.

Jerry Studdard averaged 21.6 ppg and Buck Ethridge averaged 15 ppg to lead the Rebels. In addition to his enthusiasm and personable nature, Colson was more than willing to get out and knock on doors to develop enthusiasm and interest in the Rebels.

The Rebels traveled in Ford Econoline vans, one of which was driven by Dr. Thaxton from time to time. Meals on the road were fast food and the hotel was usually the basement, locker room or stage of the gym where they were playing. No Marriott or Holiday Inn Express for these young Rebels ... they were on a tight budget.

The Rebels fight for a rebound.

Nonetheless, the young Rebels put together a promising first campaign under Coach Colson. It was the Rebels' first winning season in their five-year history. The season closed and Colson turned into a recruiter scouring the state for players from high school and junior colleges. He was searching for talented players, but more importantly those who possessed the character to develop a championship culture that reflected his competitive drive and passion. Faulkner, Parrish, Ethridge, and McIntyre would return next season, so he went in search of 5-6 players that would fit his vision of a championship culture.

1959-60: Three Steps Forward, Two Steps Back

The young Rebels were coming off their first winning season but needed a couple of new players. In stepped Jim Melvin from Plains and Jim Nichols from Valdosta. Although their paths to Valdosta were quite different, their skills, athleticism, basketball IQ, and character were those Coach Colson had been looking for.

Melvin had been a standout guard in the central Georgia area in high school and junior college, and as he says, at the time "my biggest dream was to play for Valdosta State and be the best!" He tells the story of the day he walked from his house down the dirt road

Assistant Coach Bill Grant and Coach Colson

to get the mail and in it was a letter from the Valdosta State Rebels with the Colonel logo in the left-hand corner of the envelope. As he fumbled around opening the letter, while holding his breath, it seemed like it took an eternity to open it, he says. When he read the letter, he was awestruck. Valdosta State offered him a scholarship (think Chamber of Commerce scholarship) and an opportunity to play at the school of his dreams. To this day, Melvin says, "I loved playing for Valdosta, it was the only place I wanted to play! And when that was over, it was the only place where I wanted to coach!" Coach Colson had a great playmaking guard, who was a gritty competitor, and full of passion to win! More than anything, Jim Melvin's energy and enthusiasm was evident in his hustle plays; he was a leader—an influencer with the servant leader DNA that coaches dream of having!

Nichols initially signed with and attended Vanderbilt University on a basketball scholarship. Nichols was much more than a basketball player; he was an exceptional student, majoring in chemistry. During the latter part of his first year at Vandy, while scrimmaging against the varsity, there was a loose ball that Nichols and another player went after. The collision was violent, throwing Nichols headfirst into the floor. There was a concussion, followed by emergency surgery to relieve swelling. After recovering from the surgery, there were lingering issues. The Vandy trainers and doctors said his career was over (at least for the immediate future). Nichols returned home to Valdosta to recuperate and gather himself before making any decisions. In the fall of 1959, he enrolled in Valdosta State and decided to walk-on to the basketball team, much to the distress of his parents, physician, and friends.

The 1959-60 Rebels, from left to right: John McIntyre, Charles Greene, Jim Melvin, Steve Kebler, Jim Nichols, Buck Ethridge, Doug Parrish, Max Stephens, Hansel Faulkner, Willie Hunt, and Tim Vinson.

Nichols was a determined, resilient, and rugged 6-foot-5 ball player, whose basketball IQ was outstanding. His most significant attributes on the floor were his nose for the ball off the glass, willingness to set bone-rattling picks to spring other players for easy looks at the basket, and his overall intensity. He did not know Colson, and his memory is foggy about how he made the team, along with three other Valdosta HS graduates: Charlie Greene (mgr.), John McIntyre, and Tim Vinson. Nichols says that "there weren't any scholarships, if any, they were minimal." What these young men understood was what it took to win big time games and championships. The Rebels featured a very balanced lineup night in and night out: Melvin, Faulkner, Parrish, Ethridge, and Nichols.

Parrish goes high as Faulkner follows.

Ethridge and Nichols stormed the backboards every night, as did Faulkner (and others). Although the Rebels were outmanned size-wise against the stronger opponents, their tenacity and work ethic often more than compensated for any height differential. The height disparity between the Rebels would become a familiar theme in the early 60s, although the Rebels never allowed that to determine the outcome of games in general. Their resilience, tenacity, and "will to win" every rebound battle attest to their indomitable spirit. The Rebel Spirit was evident to even the least knowledgeable fan.

Although the won-loss record was not what Colson had been looking for or expecting from his young and inexperienced team, they ended the year winning every game but one at home, further developing the home court advantage all champions have. In addition, Melvin and Nichols, two critical leaders in the locker room and on the floor, were returning next year. Lastly, Colson had broken the code on Pinholster's Wheel offense and would have it firmly installed and ready to go next season.

The ever optimistic and upbeat Gary Colson hit the road to recruit. It was time to take the next step and bring home a championship as the decade of the 60s opens.

Jim Nichols shoots against Mercer

5

1960-1964 GIAC Champions

1960-61: Third Year's a Charm

Coach Colson had spent his first two years developing the culture and enhancing the roster (as well as equipment and uniforms, etc.) as the first season of the '60s appeared on the horizon. Within that short period of time, with the enhanced recruiting (focusing on both talent and character) and the installation of the Wheel, VSC began to turn things around.

By now, Colson knew the schedule and who the rivals were in both the GIAC and the NAIA District 25. Shorter, Berry, West Georgia, and LaGrange were hurdles Valdosta State would have to jump over to become conference champions. Although Piedmont was in the GIAC, and always seemed to have size and physicality, they could never contend for a championship—but if you were not paying attention, they would beat you, especially in Demorest. The NAIA District 25 was loaded with heavy hitters like Georgia Southern under JB Scearce, Garland Pinholster's Oglethorpe squad, Jacksonville (FL) University, Stetson University under legendary Glenn Wilkes, Florida Southern, Rollins, and the University of Tampa. Georgia Southern and Oglethorpe were part of the Rebels' yearly rotation of games, whereas the Florida schools would slide on and off periodically. The Rebels also regularly faced off with Florida State University, which at this time was developing into a basketball powerhouse. The Rebels' schedule was not for the faint of heart and would require an indomitable spirit from everyone!

Pictured Front Row, from left to right: Charlie Green (asst. Coach), Roger Douglas, Mike Perry, W.A. Carver, Robert Sanders, Herman Hudson, Gary Colson (Head Coach). Second Row: Jerry Greenwald (Mgr.), Jim Melvin, Doug Winters, Jim Nichols, Sonny Williams, Bob Anderson, Homer Chambliss, Robert Bailey, and John Dalzell.

Colson hit on the recruiting front with junior college transfers Homer Chambliss, Sonny Williams, Bob Anderson, and Doug Winters; as well as a boatload of freshman—Mike Perry, Roger Douglas, Bob Sanders, Herman Hudson, and W.A. Carver. This was Colson's first freshman class.

Although Homer Chambliss was barely 6-2, he played more like 6-8. His vertical leap was never measured but could easily have been about 35-inches, which is elite leaping ability. More important, according to Colson, "Homer had a nose for the ball on every rebound! And he thought it was his, he wanted the ball really bad." Between his sixth sense, desire, and his leaping ability, he was a rebounding machine on both ends of the floor. He was literally a "force of nature on the boards!" Mike Perry says Homer was the "epitome of the phrase leaving it all on the floor! He thought every rebound was his and went after each with that attitude."

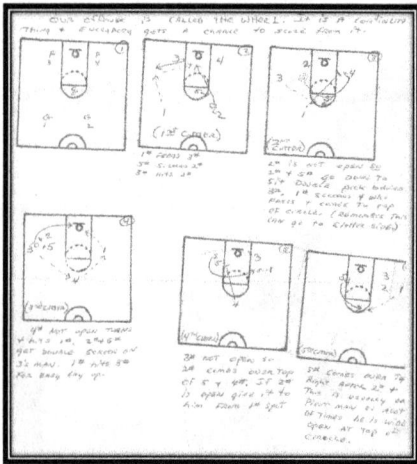

The "Wheel" Offense

Bob Anderson, a 6-6 wing player, provided the Rebels with more depth as he could shoot and score. He was a great complement to the established 6-5 Jim Nichols. Nichols and Anderson would average close to double digits in rebounds this season, as well as averaging close to double digits in points per game. Sonny Williams, a 6-6 junior from Young Harris JC, would end up starting and providing much needed scoring and rebounding depth.

Another important addition was Doug Winters, who could score points in bunches. Winters arrived from Truett-McConnell Junior College and would become a starter. Although freshman Mike Perry was an excellent "lefty shooter" his contributions this year would be minimal since Colson's tendency was to rely on upperclassmen.

A vital key to the Rebels' success would be their commitment to and execution of the Wheel offense that Colson acquired via Bill Long's film of Garland Pinholster's offense. Colson has repeatedly admitted he does not invent offenses but tries to find what is working for others and adapts it to the talent he has. His humility to accept what he has and his willingness to go find and learn a system that works elsewhere, then adapt it is exceptional. The great coaches in history have this characteristic. In this case, Colson added some "touches'" to the Wheel that were unique to Valdosta State. In so doing, Colson would eventually leap over Pinholster and Oglethorpe, but not this year.

The notes and charts on the previous page are Colson's and are reflective of the level of detail players were expected to learn and apply regarding the various cuts and motions of the vaunted Valdosta State version of the Wheel.

Doug Winters scores in the Valdosta State Gym and Jim Melvin follows up

The Wheel offensive system fit Colson's philosophy of teamwork over individual talent, as well as the talent he had recruited. As the season pressed on, the Rebels executed their offense like assassins, with devilish precision-like strikes, from either relatively uncontested layups to wide open jump shots. The Rebels played on the offensive end of the floor with a freshness and unquenchable zeal to share the ball.

The Rebels' schedule was loaded with tough teams. The Rebels lost to the likes of Rollins, Florida Southern, and Oglethorpe; but claimed wins against other non-conference foes Georgia State and College of Charleston. History was made on Feb. 2, 1961, when the Rebels beat Piedmont in Demorest, 72-61. The Rebels trailed by 10 at halftime but put their foot on the gas the last 20 minutes to outscore the Lions by 19 points led by Chambliss and Melvin.

The Rebels went undefeated in the GIAC, running the table by going 12-0 and winning their first GIAC Championship (and recording their second winning season in school history).

Chambliss would lead the Rebels with 14.4 ppg, closely followed by Winters with 14.1 ppg. In the meantime, Sonny Williams. Anderson, Nichols, and Williams were a force on the boards throughout the season.

Homer Chambliss scores as Doug Winters looks on

Named to the All GIAC first team were Melvin, Chambliss, Winters, and Williams. Winters was the best FT shooter on the team, although his form was unorthodox to some. Coach Colson asked him, "When did you start shooting free throws in the same manner you shoot a regular jump shot?" To our knowledge, Winters has not revealed the secret nor the answer.

How did Coach Colson turn the corner in only his third season at the helm? He recruited players that aligned with his philosophy, who were committed to playing through the echo of the whistle to win championships. The character and diversity of the players cannot be overstated in its influence on the results on the floor. Consider that numerous players played multiple sports (Nichols, Winters, and Perry); as well as being active in Student Life and Government (an example is Nichols: SG Treasurer, member of Sig Ep fraternity, and Who's Who).

Colson adapted and installed an offensive system that reflected his team-first philosophy and fully empowered the talent on hand. He had a locker room full of team-oriented players, who genuinely cared for and loved one another. Nichols describes this locker room: "The times were simpler, with less baggage—like the players. Most of us came from small towns and did not bring their press clippings with them. We were just guys with lots of different backgrounds and personalities that developed a camaraderie and espirit de corps that enabled us to learn how to perform as a team. We arrived from different small towns, but with similar values. And here we are, 50 years later, meeting and talking with one another the way we did when we played." Winters adds, "my teammates were team players first and foremost. We had incredible competition at practice; yet when we walked off the floor, we developed lifetime lasting relationships!"

Lastly, Colson built depth, in the face of limited funding. Colson and Coach Grant had a limited scholarship budget for each sport, which meant they had to become highly creative to land the talent needed to win championships. Players came with partial scholarships in basketball, plus tennis or baseball. Then Colson and Grant got creative. The Detroit Tigers minor league team was leaving Valdosta, which meant the field, adjacent offices, and locker rooms were available. Colson and Grant got the offices and locker rooms donated to the school and turned them into what is one of the great oral traditions in Rebel history, "The Shack." It housed up to 16 players (basketball and baseball). Perry writes, "By the end of its tenure, it was the place everyone on campus wanted to live." The coaches had taken care of the "room" of room and board, so their creativity continued onto covering meals.

Gerald Davidson ('61-'62) describes "having my meal ticket at the Hitching Post, the best hamburger place at the time. Coach Colson had engaged various restaurants to provide meals for various players. Doug Winters ate at the Plantation, an upscale restaurant, and explained to me (in jest) that the restaurant indicated the 'pecking order' of the team. However, I did eat the best hamburger in Valdosta!" Coach Colson had hit the streets enlisting the help of the community to meet the needs of the up-and-coming program. In usual and customary fashion, the Valdosta community jumped on board with both feet! After all, Valdosta knew what it takes to win championships!

History had been made by the young Rebels, a GIAC Championship and becoming the first team in the conference to run the table, 12-0. Coach Colson's excellence shined through because of the mysterious process by which he was able to stir his players to reach their potential as individuals and as a team. He had been able to set standards and apply them, and manage a diverse group of egos, eventually getting them from me to us. The saying "the proof is in the pudding" fits. The Rebels were Champions!

As winter turned to spring, Colson looked at his roster for the next season and saw he had six lettermen returning. Expectations were high, with the potential for Back-to-Back championships looming!

1961-62: Back-to-Back GIAC Championships?

Lou Holtz was known as a coach who took numerous football programs from the basement to a championship. Holtz's developmental process goes like this: 1) He says players must learn how to win and finish ("play through the echo of the whistle") the first five minutes of the first quarter, then the next five minutes, and finally learn how to close the quarter out and win the quarter. 2) Then they must learn how to do the same with the first half, then the second half. 3) Then they must learn how to close out games in that manner. 4) Learn how to win games at home and then on the road. 5) Only then can they begin to aspire to a conference championship. 6) Once the conference championship is in hand, then they add the national championship to their objectives.

Likewise, Colson had brought the young Rebels through the fires of losing during his first two seasons, but there were powerful lessons learned in those moments. By the third season, the Rebels were mentally and physically prepared to set their sights on the GIAC Championship and literally steamrolled through the season. They went undefeated in the GIAC and had not lost a conference game at home in two years.

What challenges does a coach face following a championship season, especially the first in school history? Like Holtz, Pat Riley knew and addressed the real issue or challenge of attempting to go back-to-back: "When the championship is achieved, the quest for validation tends to shift to other pursuits. It's a natural problem, one born of winning's diminishing returns. Even the greatest competitors can only dredge up so much motivation to keep going after victory alone. The Bulls were fantastic at suppressing the Disease of Me, but between Pippen and Rodman, they saw flare-ups of individual angst. As a team, they were successful at managing something that has no known cure, and nearly always, wins eventually." As season four approached, Colson's biggest challenge might not be the daunting schedule but what was in the heads and hearts within the team.

Although he had six solid players returning from last year's squad, Colson was uneasy as the proverbial "cat on a hot tin roof" after an early season blowout of Alabama Christian, in which sophomore sensation Mike Perry scored 26 points. He told Sammy Glassman "he was pleased, but not completely satisfied" with the execution and effort the team displayed during the game. Colson continued, "we won our opener, which is pleasing, but we have a long way to go......We are going to have to make a lot of improvements on both ends of the court going forward." Colson was expressing his concern that there was not a great deal of continuity from last year's group to this team, because he brought on six new players. He was acknowledging what every coach understands—each new season requires a new team chemistry to be formed, which can make a coach lose lots of sleep. Later in the article, he acknowledged he had key players returning and he was encouraged so far, saying "I just hope it's a sign they are going to make steady improvement this year."

He was in good hands with his leadership from the returning lettermen: Jim Nichols, Mike Perry, Doug Winters, Bob Anderson, and

Robert Bailey! While height might be an issue, this group brought a temperament that consisted of a powerful will to win, a fiery competitive spirit, relentless resolve, and never-ending level of resilience. They were unafraid and in fact looked forward to big challenges as opportunities! Not only did the Rebels have lots of character and the "Rebel Spirit" returning, but these were talented ball players. On the inside, the Rebels had Jim Nichols, Bob Anderson, and Robert Bailey. Out front was All Conference Doug Winters, plus Herman Hudson and sophomore Mike Perry. Colson had not had this much talent and experience returning in his tenure. Again, he recruited some great players and people that fit the culture and schemes in Angie Devivo, Preston Hodges, Marcus Shipman, Gerald Davidson, and Bill Summerford.

This group of Rebels quickly captured the hearts and minds of the student body and community. They played unselfishly, and it was obvious they were there for their teammates, reflecting joy in delivering a pass to an open teammate, who showed a sincere gratitude for the pass. They never failed to "come to play" and were always around the ball on defense, swarming like South Georgia gnats in the heat of summer. If the ball hit the floor, at least two Rebels were in hot pursuit, leaving precious skin on the varnished floor. They literally left everything they had on the floor every night!

The Rebels had not lost a conference game at home in two years, so Rebel Nation took lots of pride in their impact on the game by creating noise that would be "oceanic" in a sense, enveloping the players with wave after wave of intense enthusiasm. Every new moment in the game elicited a louder, more vociferous, and magnificent level of energy and noise. The crowd was as if they were one cyclonic voice that lifted the Rebels' energy to levels where they would be willing to literally take on Goliath (FSU or UNC or UK)!

As the season opened, it was evident that Colson had, in three short years, developed the "Rebel Tradition," which Perry later eloquently described when he wrote, "Tradition can't be bought; it must be earned. The process usually takes several years to take root and could carry a team for years once established. We recognize great teams when their name is mentioned (see the Prologue). Those teams expected to win when they took the court and played accordingly. Between 1961 and 1972, the Valdosta State Rebels developed and maintained such a tradition! They won because winning was a by-product of doing the fundamental things the right way (thanks Wright Bazemore)—which is something the Rebels excelled at doing!"

Front Row, left to right: Coach Gary Colson, Angie Devivo, Robert Bailey, Jim Nichols, Bob Anderson, Preston Hodges, Mike Perry, Coach Charlie Greene. Second Row: Tommy Thomas (Manager), Marcus Shipman, Herman Hudson, Roger Douglas, Bill Summerford, Doug Winters, Gerald Davidson, and Jerry Norman (Manager).

What the 1961-62 Rebels did still stands as the greatest season in school history, going 19-2 and 12-0 in the GIAC for the second year in a row!

Following is a summary of the key battles along the journey to Back-To-Back GIAC Championships:

- The Rebels beat the College of Charleston two times within 10 days before Christmas, trouncing them in Charleston by 21 points. The dreaded injury bug raised its ugly head in Charleston as Robert Bailey reinjured his knee and was unavailable. Colson simply turned Gerald Davidson loose on their leading scorer; the result was their guy scored 1 point! To describe the 5-10 Davidson as a bulldog on the defensive end is an understatement. Gerald vividly remembers the Christmas card he received over the Christmas break from Colson that said, "Great job on Polis!" More importantly, he describes how much he enjoyed feasting on the hamburger steak after the game. Colson awarded this treat to those players who drew offensive fouls! Winters, Perry, and Anderson continued to lead the Rebels in scoring, and Nichols was consistently coming down with double digits in rebounds.

- In Rome, Georgia, the Rebels found themselves down 13 points to Berry, 39-26, with 10 minutes left in the game and point guard Angie Devivo on the bench with four fouls. Colson called time out, put in mighty-mite Gerald Davidson

Georgia Five Wins In Last 8 Seconds

By JACK SLAYTON
Ledger Sports Editor

Those closing seconds proved fatal to the Florida Southern College Mocs again last night at the Lakeland High gym for the second straight evening as Valdosta State took a come-from-behind 53-52 victory from the Mocs.

The loss was the second in a row Southern has suffered in the closing seconds—Transylvania beating them Friday, 64-63. It came on a drive down the middle and a layup by Valdosta's Doug Winters in the final eight seconds of the game.

and went to a 1-3-1 trap. The Rebels put their foot on the gas pedal once again when the chips were down, winning going away 51-44. Winters had 17, Perry 15, and Anderson 10. Nichols recorded another double-digit rebound night, capturing 16 caroms off the glass.

- Rebels 53, Florida Southern 52. The Rebels went into Lakeland, FL and took the game right to the vaunted Moccasins. It was the Rebels' first win of a highly respected opponent on the road in the history of the school! As the seesaw affair wound down, Winters stole the ball and went the length of the court for the game-winning layup (left-handed) in the last 8 seconds for the win!
- The Rebels swept the season series from the central Florida powers, beating Rollins in Orlando 59-43 (and having beat FL Southern).

- The Rebels rolled into Demorest to play Piedmont with an unblemished record in the GIAC, 11-0. Piedmont has always been one of those teams that could pull off an upset if an opportunity presented itself. Not against these "rampaging" Rebels, who pulled out a 53-52 nail-biter to go undefeated in the conference for the second year in a row.

Rollins' Phil Hurt (41) Drives For Goal
Finds Valdosta State's Doug Winters (22) In His Way

The 1961-62 version of the Rebels was a relentless defensive juggernaut, which fueled this unprecedented second undefeated run through the conference! The Rebels were the sixth-best defense in the nation within the NAIA, limiting teams to 55 ppg. They were ranked in the Top 10 offensively in FT at 76.5% and FG at 49.7%.

Gerald Davidson says he believes "with the Rebels running the Wheel, it created a feeling of team first. With Mike and Doug leading the offensive attack; Jim, Robert, and Bob hitting the boards, setting killer screens and scoring when the opportunity presented itself; along with Angie Devivo and myself contributing defensively and setting up the offense; it was difficult for any team to stay with us." The Rebels had matured right in front of everyone's eyes. They were now doing the hunting and winning. Davidson goes further, describing the culture within the Rebel program, "a characteristic that comes to mind was unselfishness and teamwork. We ran an offensive system in which everyone had a role to play and we stayed in our lane, took care of our responsibilities.

We knew who our offensive players were, our rebounders, playmakers, and defensive players. This showed up in every game. At the end of the day, we pulled for and cared about one another."

The season was one for the ages! A third-straight season sweeping conference foes at home, winning the last 29 conference games in a row, winning a back-to-back GIAC Championship, and winning 19 of 21 games (still a school record). The only blemishes on the record was a 30-point loss at Florida State and a tough loss to NAIA power Cumberland College (KY) toward the end of the season.

The honors for the Rebels rolled in:

- Winters, Perry, and Nichols were named All GIAC. Winters for the second year in a row.
- Winters was named MVP by the coaching staff.
- Nichols was the Best FG % and Rebel Spirit Award winner.
- Anderson was named Most Improved and won the FT % award.
- Devivo was named Best Play Maker.
- Davidson was named Best Defender.
- Colson was named Coach of the Year in the GIAC for the second year in a row.

A number of players went on to spring sports. Tommy Thomas (basketball manager) won MVP for the Rebel baseball squad. Winters played tennis. Nichols and Winters were Student Body leaders and worked in fraternities and clubs through-out the year.

Nichols was leaving Valdosta State after three years of incredible contributions on the court, in the classroom, and on campus. He was selected to Who's Who and graduated with honors with a degree in Chemistry. This was no small task since his Chemistry professor told Colson that Nichols cannot play basketball and major in chemistry at the same time and proceeded to make sure it was difficult for him. If you know Nichols, you know how he dealt with such a challenge, head on and full speed! He is the epitome of the "Rebel Spirit" Award which he won. On the court, he left a legacy that would continue until Valdosta State left the GIAC for the NCAA. Nichols says "the bonds I made with Lovey Anderson and Homer Chambliss were special, even sacred in a manner of speaking. When a person is in the middle of their

playing career, it is hard to realize the full effect of what they are doing until later in time. Looking back today and viewing the string of
GIAC Championships—while every conference opponent had circled
the date on their schedule to make sure they were the ones to knock off
the vaunted Rebels—is quite an accomplishment. More importantly, I
met my wife of 57 years, Sunny, at Valdosta State."

Winters left Valdosta State as a
two-time GIAC All-Conference
player, and MVP in 1961-62. He
would go on to earn a Ph.D. and
become a School Superintendent.
Winters remembers the game-
winning layup against Florida
Southern, as well as "the great pro-
fessors, excellent student center,
and beautiful campus." Furthermore, he said, "the friendships we
developed among the players (and
with other students) during these
years are special. Those relationships continue today, from 50
years ago."

Stress of Game Shows In Jim Nichols' Face
Valdosta State Center Goes Up to Score Fiel Goal

Davidson departed Valdosta State after one year, but it was memorable to the mighty-mite. "I am so grateful to be a part of this legacy!
All the GIAC Championships, the outstanding records, the special 19-2
season; but above all else having lasting relationships with Coach Colson and my teammates." Gerald noted that he and Winters worked
together within the Hall County School System, Winters as Superintendent and Davidson as Associate Superintendent.

Colson never rested on his laurels. He was always seeking out players
who fit and had good to great talent. Next season, the Rebels would be
without stalwarts Winters, Davidson, and Nichols. So as spring '62 unfolded, Colson hit the recruiting trails in Georgia to discover more tal-

ent to go along with a solid nucleus of Perry, Devivo, Hudson, Hodges, and Summerford.

Was there a Three-Peat blowing through the South Georgia pines at Valdosta State?

1962-63: *Three-Peats Put a Team in Rare Air*

At any level of athletics, winning three championships in a row is rare! Consider the Jordan-era Bulls won six titles in eight years from 1990 to 1998, including not one, but two, three-peats! The Boston Celtics, the gold standard for professional sports dynasties, won an amazing 11 championships in 13 seasons, including eight titles in a row from to 1959 to 1966. Here are the NBA Three-Peats:

- 1952–1954 Minneapolis Lakers
- 1959–1966 Boston Celtics (8)
- 1991–1993 Chicago Bulls
- 1996–1998 Chicago Bulls
- 2000–2002 Los Angeles Lakers

Consider that the great Showtime Lakers (1979-1991) who won five titles and appeared in nine finals over a 12-season run, never had a three-peat. And no team has accomplished the coveted three-peat since the Shaq/Kobe Lakers (2000-2002).

Winning three titles in a row in any conference or professional league is difficult for a myriad of reasons: untimely injuries, schedules, parity, age, continuity of leadership, etc. Michael Jordan and the Bulls did it twice, which cemented their legacy as one of the best teams in NBA history and Jordan as the GOAT in basketball. However, the road to winning three championships in a row was not easy. Jordan said his biggest challenge was to achieve something Larry Bird or Magic Johnson never did. "After we won the first two titles back to back, the only reason I came back was to win three in a row, which was something

Larry and Magic never did. That was my only motivation. I was tired ... just fed up with all of the politics within the locker room ... Phoenix was no problem, at least compared to New York ...winning a third-straight championship was the hardest thing I've ever done on the basketball court."

Front Row, left to right: Edgar Greene (Mgr.), Gary Colson, Jerry Norman (Mgr.), Bo Spence, Marcus Shipman (GA) Second row: Ray McCully, Angie Devivo, Herman Hudson, Dennis Fike, Bobby Ritch, Bob Speck, Tommy Johnson Third Row: Preston Hodges, Roger Douglas, Bill Summerford, Wally Summers, Chuch Bonavitch, Bill Brinson, Austin DeLoach, Mike Perry

Colson had developed a deeper bench after he began adding freshman recruits in the fall of 1960. Consequently, in October of '62, he saw familiar faces show up for practice: Mike Perry (Jr.), Angie Devivo (Sr.), Herman Hudson (Jr.), Preston Hodges (Soph.), Roger Douglas (Jr.), and Bill Summerford (Sr.). Perry was an All-Conference guard who could shoot the lights out.

The new recruits were;

- Ray McCully had completed his four year enlistment commitment to the Marines and had two opportunities to go play college ball and earn a degree. One of those opportunities was Valdosta State. He and his wife chose Valdosta. The 5-10 point guard had played four years of service ball, so he was not a young 17-year-old, but a seasoned veteran who had been through leadership training and was ready to go from the outset. Mike Perry and Bobby Ritch both have said that "you had better have your head up and your eyes on Ray because he could see slivers of openings in which to pass the ball, and it was coming in hot." Ray would be known for his powerful will, fiery competitiveness, and ability to get the shooters the ball when and where they wanted it!

- Wally Summers was a transfer from Georgia Tech via ABAC. He was a brawler and a scorer. He had a hair trigger temper that often landed him on the bench, while on other occasions fueled his energy to chase down loose balls and rebound. He loved to shoot, and could shoot, which was a great thing; because now the Rebels could put two men on the floor who could shoot the lights out: Summers and Perry.

Ray McCully

- Chuck Bonovitch was a "load" at 6-6, 215 pounds. He transferred from Georgia Southern (as well as playing while he was in the Marines) and brought with him an unbelievable amount of guts and heart, which made him a force on the glass. Chuck would become known for throwing his body at every rebound and loose ball for the Rebels. He astonished most big men he played against with his relentless approach to rebounding. Colson had found the man to replace Nichols in the paint!

- Tommy Johnson was a team-first guard who went for every loose ball, giving everything his body had to give, was a solid playmaker, and had great basketball IQ. He also was an excellent baseball player.

- Bobby Ritch was another true Freshman who could have been playing at Ole Miss or other major programs. Jerry Studdard spoke to Ritch in Homerville over lunch one day after a city league basketball game. Studdard asked if Ritch wanted him to get him a tryout at Valdosta State. Elroy Griffis, a mutual friend, said he would

Chuck Bonovitch

get Ritch there if Studdard got the tryout. The tryout was set up, which at that time consisted of some scrimmaging, but more importantly playing Colson one-on-one. Colson was in his early 30s, but was still cat quick, extremely skilled, and an extremely intense competitor. Ritch beat the coach, which did not happen often in these contests. Colson offered him the scholarship on the spot. In the 6-2 Ritch, the Rebels had a legitimate "generational" player, which is why he was recruited by SEC schools. Ritch could handle and shoot the ball; more importantly, he could create his own shot. He would take the other team's best player and shut him down. He also would crash the glass and give his body up for loose balls. This is yet another example of synchronicity or fate, where a lunch ends up landing a recruit. It is another example of the loyalty Colson's former players have toward him. It will go down as one of the great recruiting "gets" in Colson's illustrious history, nonetheless, but not the last.

Bobby Rich, Preston Hodges, Chuck Bonovitch, Mike Perry and Ray McCully

Getting the returning players and the new recruits from "me to us" would be one of Colson's primary tasks as practice started. Yet there were hidden advantages beneath the surface with this group. Devivo, McCully, and Bonovitch were older (early 20s) players, having served and played ball in the military before enrolling in school. Also, the Rebels had four players who were married; consequently, the fact was Colson added age, experience, and maturity to a veteran group of returning players. Colson's bench would be at least 9-10 deep. Colson's primary objective of team building would be essential for this group to accomplish the cherished Three-Peat!

The team building got off on the right foot from the beginning. McCully noted that "without exception my teammates welcomed a nontraditional (married) student like myself."

Part of Colson's team-building process was the training and development that freshmen would need to undergo. Colson's game management style was not to put anyone on the floor until he was 100% sure they are ready to go, which meant understanding the system and your responsibilities, as well as displaying that Rebel Spirit. That meant freshman usually spent the first year learning. Colson was always known as a great teacher of the game, but a tradition he implemented at Valdosta State was that upperclassmen were expected to help educate new recruits in the nuances of the systems and core values of the Rebel Tradition.

As preseason workouts wound down, with the start of the season right around the corner, Colson settled on the starters: McCully, Hodges, Perry, Summers, and Bonovitch. Although three of the starters were new, they had lots of maturity and game experience (and they were exceptionally talented).

Sammy Glassman, Sports Editor for the Valdosta Daily Times, spoke to Colson as he was developing his preseason outlook piece for the paper. Glassman wrote that "when I arrived in 1960, some folks who are close to the local sports scene said Valdosta is not a 'basketball town.'" He continued, pointing out that "Coach Gary Colson and his Valdosta State Rebels have proved this untrue." He noted how not only the students and staff, but the community at large have responded to the unprecedented success with selling out the gym consistently. Glassman, in his usual understated manner, writes "the VSC students turn out in full force. While they leave mechanical noise makers at home, they provide strong and enthusiastic vocal support to the Rebs." Danny Dee, the voice of the Rebels on local radio, could be heard describing the atmosphere in the sold-out gym with phrases like: "this place is shaking, the lights may fall, you can cut the intensity in this place with a knife, I can't hear myself think much less talk, I'm hearing Wilbert Harrison warming up on the stage—I think we're headed to Kansas City baby!" Colson had turned a young, unknown program into a rampaging Rebel force to be reckoned with; and "Winnerville" residents as well as the students and staff were on board!

It's time to "lace 'em up and get after it!" Here are the highlights from another season of Rebel Basketball:

• The season began with uneven performances, although the opening schedule was tough. The Rebels pummeled Berry but turned right around and lost to Shorter 52-40. The Rebels blasted Alabama Christian and Rollins, but got buried by Florida Southern and FSU (both on the road). They were 3-3 for the season at that point, while working on polishing the Wheel and defining a team identity. As anyone who has played basketball at a high level knows, team identity takes time to develop; it cannot be microwaved by the coach, staff, or players.

Team identity goes hand-in-hand with confidence. This Rebels squad, with three new starters, had faced FSU, Florida Southern, Rollins, Berry, and Shorter on the road. They had gone 2-3 in that group of road contests. That is a tough road to travel for any team, although the coach will find out what they are made of—are they resilient and relentless?

There is a great piece of wisdom that fits this team at this moment in their season-

"it's darkest before the dawn"

• The Rebels had four games left before the GIAC conference schedule kicked into high gear in January: Georgia State, the Oglethorpe Christmas Tournament, and the College of Charleston. The Oglethorpe Tournament first round foe was Georgetown (KY) College, a well-known NAIA powerhouse that had been to the NAIA National Tournament in Kansas City five-straight years—always considered capable of winning it. Valdosta State had never knocked off such a team in its brief history, a fact Coach Colson used to challenge the Rebels before they left for Atlanta. The light came on as they took the floor to face the Georgetown Tigers. The Atlanta Constitution noted that "matching unrestrained determination with a complementing number of baskets, gritty Valdosta State shot majestically into the final round of the Oglethorpe Invitational Basketball Tournament on Monday night." Although the Tigers had a 7-point lead at the half, the Rebels elevated the defensive intensity, and "resolutely went about flooring the heavily favored Kentuckians."

Mike Perry (13), Preston Hodge (14), and Wally Summers (30)

The charge was led by Bonovitch, "a hulking 6-6 transfer from Georgia Southern who took it upon himself to" take over the paint, clearing the boards of every rebound in the gym. The Rebels tied the game with 6:28 left at 54-54, controlling the Tigers and the game from that point forward, winning 64-54. The Rebels outscored Georgetown 38-21 in the second half.

It was the defensive effort that served as the catalyst for the win, but take a look at the balanced scoring from the Rebels: Bonovitch had 16 (plus 9 rebounds), Perry had 16, and Summers and Hodges both had 13, and Mc-Cully had 6. Georgetown's All American Dick Vories, who had 18 in the first half, would be held to 9 in the second half. While the Rebels lost to Oglethorpe the next night in the championship game, they were returning home confident in their team identity, as well as confident they could step onto the floor with anyone, anywhere! The Rebels blew by Charleston in Valdosta, making them 6-5 as they entered the conference season.

- The Rebels opened the conference season against Berry and Shorter in Valdosta. They routed Berry by 22, holding them to 44 points, and won a hard fought defensive contest against Shorter,

43-42. Then they hit the road in those Ford Econoline vans to La-Grange and Carrollton. They rampaged through West Georgia, winning by 14 (holding the Braves to 49), but the wheels came off in LaGrange, losing 87-63. The Rebels were not used to losing to conference foes, regardless of whether it was a preseason game or conference game; they had lost to Shorter earlier in a preseason tournament and now LaGrange. Remember, the Rebels had gone undefeated in the GIAC two consecutive seasons, plus winning their last five conference games in row the season before that. Although the Rebels were 3-1 in the GIAC, the next four conference games would tell Colson a lot more about the level of resilience and relentlessness of this team as they would face off with LaGrange, Piedmont, Berry, and Shorter. As the Rebels had done in December before taking down Georgetown, they rallied as champions have the tendency to do and brought an elevated energy onto the floor the remainder of the season. They easily handled Piedmont and LaGrange in Valdosta, then split in Rome by beating Berry in OT by one, then losing a hard fought game with the Hawks, 60-57, without Wally Summers, whose wife had given birth to a baby girl that day. The Rebels' GIAC record stood at 6-2, with two games to go.

• Into the middle of this intense moment stepped the powerful FSU Seminoles, which had agreed to make a trip to Valdosta this season. The first game in Tallahassee was a 30-point blowout in favor of the 'Noles. The gym was beyond capacity, with people literally sitting on the stage and the overhang above the entry doors. The atmosphere was electric, with legendary PA announcer Red Cross doing his best to incite a riot among the Rebel Nation; aided by the Rebel cheerleaders! You could have cut the intensity with a knife in the locker room as the team exited to climb the stairs to the floor. What an effort the Rebels put forth! The lead changed hands 17 times, neither team gaining a decided advantage or momentum.

The crowd noise continued to rise with each possession! The game would come down to a final trip down the floor by the Rebels with 15 seconds left, trailing by two. Close, but no cigars were forthcoming on this rainy night in Georgia. The Rebels fell short, 61-56. Again, the outmanned squad showed they could compete with anyone, anywhere because of that resilient and relentless Rebel Spirit. The Rebels had a bal-

Hodges (14), Summers, and Ritch (22) vs. FSU.

anced scoring attack that night as well; led by Bonovitch with 13, Summers 12, Perry 9, Hodges 8, Ritch 8, and McCully 6. FSU won the battle of the boards 29-22, but the game turned at the FT line, where FSU was 12-for-15 and the Rebels went 8-for-14.

- The Rebels would finish off their conference schedule with wins over West Georgia and Piedmont to finish 8-2, tied with Shorter College (who had beaten Valdosta State 2 out of 3 already this season). A Championship playoff game was scheduled to be played in Macon at Mercer University's gym. (A quick note to remind everyone that Colson won a state championship in high school at Macon. The basketball gods were smiling on the Rebels when the conference said play this game in Macon!) This game was played the way "win or go home championship games" are supposed to be played—maximum effort for 45 minutes (OT). Every player on both squads left everything they had on the floor. According to the Associated Press account of the game, "to say that Valdosta State was ready to play for the all the marbles is an understatement. Coach Gary Colson had his Rebels fired up to spectacular proportions" and they used that energy to take a 41-34 halftime lead. The Rebels were off and running thanks to the shooting of Perry and Summers. Shorter's All-Conference stud, Gordon Guinn, led a breathtaking comeback in the second half. Guinn scored 28 points for the night. The game headed to OT with the score knotted at 70. With the score tied at 76, Guinn was bringing the ball down the floor for a possible last shot attempt for Shorter. Freshman Bobby Ritch saw him glance at the clock and the cat quick Ritch stole the ball and made the layup that enabled the Rebels to win their third consecutive GIAC Championship, 78-76. Scoring for the playoff with Shorter went like this: Perry 29, Summers 20, Ritch 11, Hodges 6, Bonovitch and McCully 5 each, and Summerford 2. Up to this season, the Shorter-Valdosta State rivalry was somewhat subdued, but Shorter beat the Rebels two out of three times during the season and had expected to win their third in this playoff game. Yet the Rebels found a way to prevail yet again, shattering Shorter's dreams and visions of a GIAC Championship. The Shorter rivalry would heat up in the coming years under the direction of Coach Bill Foster; nonetheless, the road to the GIAC Championship ran through "Titletown!"

• The next mountain peak for the Rebels to climb was to win the NAIA District 25 Championship. The Rebels headed to Jacksonville for the NAIA District 25 Tournament to play JU (host) in the first round. Stetson and Georgia Southern were matched in the other side of the bracket. The three other teams in the tournament had been to this dance frequently and were all highly regarded in the small college circle of championship contenders. All three had at least one outstanding player; JU had 6-5 Roger Strickland (unanimous NAIA All American), Southern had 6-5 Jim Sealey, and Stetson had 6-7 Lamar Deaver (who was averaging a double double). These teams were coached by men who would become legends: Glenn Wilkes (Stetson) and JB Scearce (Georgia Southern). This tournament would be a challenge for all four teams. The moment of truth for the season had come, and for the Rebel program not quite 10 years old, a chance to leap another hurdle—a District Championship. Alas, JU, Roger Strickland, and the home court advantage proved too much for the Rebels in this contest, winning a close game 68-62. Strickland was too much on this night, in his gym. The Rebels were led by McCully (15 points and 5 steals) and Mike Perry (20 points). Both were named to the All-Tournament Team.

It is never satisfying to lose the last game of the season, much less the first round of a postseason national tournament game! As a matter of fact, it is heart-wrenching. Pat Conroy shares that "loss invites reflection, reformulating, and a change in strategies. It hurts, bleeds, and aches. It follows you home, then seemingly calls out your name in the middle of the night. It taunts you at breakfast the next morning," and definitely sits in the frontal lobe while you are in the gym preparing for the next go round during the off-season.

Reflections of the season show that the Rebels:

- Were the first GIAC team to complete a Three-Peat, by winning the GIAC Championship after discarding Shorter (again)!
- Incorporated three new starters into the lineup, which on its own is no small feat at any level. Most pundits and analysts would call this a major rebuilding project. All Colson did was find a way to get this diverse group from "me" to "us" by late January. The Rebels found their team identity, going 10-3 from January through the playoff game with Shorter.
- Beat highly ranked and respected Georgetown (KY) in Atlanta, their first victory over a highly rated team. The Rebels turned right around and played FSU to a virtual standstill, losing 61-56 at "Titletown." The confidence gained could be seen in the District 25 first round game at Jacksonville, where it was evident to everyone the Rebels belonged on the floor with any of the other three teams.
- Floor Leadership provided by the players was incredible. As it

turned out, McCully was the mature point guard who was the glue for the team. Perry, Bonovitch, Hodges, and Summers were experienced warriors. Ritch was a great athlete, a fiery competitor, and remarkable basketball player who played beyond his years. These guys were all CHAMPIONS in every way, and it was reflected in their determination, resilience, and relentlessness over the course of the season. They won on the defensive end of the floor, where they were able to impose their will on other teams. Their collective competitive desire was reflected by their body language and actions on the defensive end, from diving for loose balls to fighting for rebounds like a Siberian tiger leaping for a meal. All they did was continue to find a way to win as a team, playing through the echo of the whistle!

- The offensive system, the Wheel, produced balanced scoring (again): Perry (13.7), Summers (13.1), Bonovitch (10.1), Hodges (9.5), Ritch (7.5), and McCully (5.2). Rebounding was evenly split between: Bonovitch (159), Summers (130), Hodges (120), Perry (93), Ritch (87), and McCully (57).
- GIAC All-Conference Honors went to Bonovitch and Summers. Bonovitch was named to the Atlanta Journal All State College Team (primarily for his play against Georgetown and Oglethorpe in December).

Upon returning, a number of Rebels went straight to the baseball diamond: Jerry Norman, Bobby Speck, Wally Summers, Mike Perry, Tommy Johnson, Herman Hudson, Preston Hodges, Bobby Ritch, and Marcus Shipman. Coach Bill Grant had turned the Rebels into contenders in baseball as well as basketball. It was not unusual in this era for athletes to play multiple sports, especially since they could receive more scholarship money. As we mentioned earlier, Colson and Grant could offer partial scholarships in both sports, which would end up covering tuition and books. Since they had put together a dorm, "The Shack," then room was covered. They covered food through various restaurants allowing athletes to eat free. These coaches were creative problem solvers to say the very least. One thing for sure, they made sure the players were taken care of in all areas!

As Coach Colson looked toward the next season, he knew he had a solid nucleus returning in seniors Perry, Bonovitch, and Hudson; junior Hodges; and sophomores McCully, Johnson, Fike, and Ritch. He began the search for a few new faces to fill out the roster and continue building for the future. The next opportunity to face the young head coach and his 1963-64 squad was climbing into rare air for any team—the possibility of a Four-Peat!

1963-64: Four-Peats are Extremely Rare!

When Colson arrived in the spring of '58, no one had a vision of a Four-Peat on the radar screen, much less the horizon. Yet in less than six years, in the spring of 1963, the Rebels sat on ledge where they could see the Four-Peat mountaintop.

Ask yourself who was the last college or professional team to win four titles in a row? Yep, it is tough to find those teams, even with the help of Google. The UCLA Bruins won seven titles in a row in the late 60s. The UConn women's basketball team won four in row in the 2010s. UNC Women's Soccer won nine National Championships in a row in the 80s-90s. Gonzaga accomplished two Four-Peats in the West Coast Conference in the early 2000s, and then won six championships in a row in the 2010s. In the world of college athletics, it is very difficult to repeat since roster turnover occurs from season to season, the parity at every level is elevated, the injury bug can bite at any moment, and scheduling—getting the right games at home can be difficult.

Winning four in a row at the professional level is next to improbable, if not impossible in the 21st century. Why were the 60s Celtics able to win eight NBA Championships in row? First, they had continuity from the bench and on the floor. They played with essentially the same roster for most of their run (Russell, Cousy, Havlicek, Howell, etc.), and the same coach, Red Auerbach. Second, they avoided major injuries. Third, they played a smaller number of playoff games. In today's NBA, many analysts believe the Bulls' two Three-Peats are as impressive as the entire Celtics' run of 11 titles due to the fact of the rosters change every couple of years, the extended regular season and playoff schedule, the parity in the league at the time, and an elevated injury factor due to fatigue.

The key factors to a four-peat are continuity of leadership (both Bench and Floor), intensional scheduling in order to manage parity, avoiding the injury bug, and winning a couple of games each year you have no business winning. You can call that luck, but Branch Rickey of the Dodgers said, "luck is the residue of design." Whether that design is in the character and/or the talent of the players recruited to fit into a system does not matter. What matters is that champions have a knack for finding a way to win!

Although the GIAC is not the NBA or NCAA D-1, that does not mean winning four conference championships would be any easier. Although the Rebels had rampaged through the conference in the early 60s, Shorter and LaGrange sent shots across the bow of the Rebels' juggernaut last season. Shorter split the four-game set with the Rebels and LaGrange held onto home court advantage. It was clear both were not going to sit idle while the Rebels ascended one championship mountaintop after another.

The biggest challenge to winning a fourth consecutive championship was making sure there was continuity with Floor Leadership. The Bench Leadership, Colson, was entering his sixth season. As such, his system and philosophy were firmly in place. He recruited talented players who could execute his system, and who, more importantly, embraced and reflected the Rebel Spirit. The recruiting began paying dividends this particular year as the key core players from the previous Championship season returned.

Front row (L-R): Mike Perry. Bill Hearn, Bill Strong, Herman Hudson, Ray McCully, Tommy Johnson. Second Row: Chester Dubberly, Ben Bates, Dennis Fike, Bobby Ritch, Tommy Mullins, Preston Hodges. Third Row: Billy Gillis, Tom Stuckey, Chuck Bonovitch, Tommy MacFarland, Gary Colson, Jimmy Hunt

New additions to this edition of the Rebels were: Bill Hearn, Bill Strong, Chester Dubberly, Tommy Mullins, Ben Bates, and Tommy McFarland. Coach Colson's management style was such that unless first-year players demonstrated through their attitude, efforts, and performance at practice they deserved playing time, it would be limited otherwise. His thoughts about this group were clear in this quote from the Valdosta Daily Times: "The new additions are a fine group of talented players who are gaining experience for the time when they would be veterans. They have shown lots of hustle and determination while getting adjusted to college ball and a new team. It's going to be hard keeping them out of the lineup next year."

As the Rebels approached the first game of the season, Coach shared these thoughts with Sammy Glassman about his perspective of the team and season: "We have got a little bit of experience, but we lack height and depth is a question mark right now. We are playing our toughest schedule and our conference is tougher than ever. We certainly cannot take anything for granted. Even the opener with Willard Tate's Alabama Christian Eagles is going to be tough and we'll have to be ready." Colson acknowledged that the GIAC (Shorter, LaGrange, and West Georgia) "are loaded." All of those teams, as well as NCAA D-2 Oglethorpe, would have a decided height advantage when they lined up against the Rebels. The cagey head coach then acknowledged that "although we are somewhat hindered by this, our team has a spirit that enables them to find ways to win games and that goes a long way in this sport!"

Coach Colson was right. This journey through the GIAC would be unlike any of the recent seasons. The Rebels would go 7-3 and play Shorter in yet another Championship Playoff game. Overall, the Rebels went 15-6.

Time to roll through the season highlights:

- The non-conference schedule included Oglethorpe (two games), the vaunted Phillips 66 Oilers AAU team (made up of former college all stars), Alabama Christian, Florida Presbyterian, St. Paul (MN), Frederick, and Taylor University. The Rebels finished this segment of the schedule 5-3, losing a heartbreaker to Oglethorpe in Valdosta, 57-55.
- This edition of the Rebels would continue to build their identity around a stingy defense, which in turn fueled a solid running game. The Rebels consistently held teams to less than 60 points during the season and would run in a heartbeat given a chance. Against non-conference foes, the Rebels scored 79, 73, 72, 85, and 86 points.

"All hands on the deck" after a loose ball vs. Oglethorpe, including Mike Perry, #25.

A great example is the game vs. Taylor University's Trojans (IN) in early January. The Trojans came into the contest averaging north of 90 points a game. Their vaunted fast-break offense was stifled by the Rebels' defensive efforts, which triggered an offensive explosion by the Rebels. In fact, senior Mike Perry lit up the scoreboard and the nets with a 37-point outburst! The Rebels knocked down 53% of their field goals, 80% at the FT line and won the rebounding battle 39-29 (not bad for a team with no one taller than 6-5).

Colson referred to this effort as "our best overall performance of the season." The Rebels again featured some balanced scoring—even with Perry's 37, Ritch had 23, Bonovitch 14, Johnson 7, and Hodges 5. Hodges led the Rebels on the glass with 11. Sophomore Tommy Johnson started in Ray McCully's place (scratched cornea) and played a solid game at point guard with silky smooth ball handling, while playing stifling defense.

• Shorter College brought in a talented young coach, Bill Foster, the year before. Foster was no slouch nor sluggard; he would go on to rebuild Clemson and the University of Miami among other national programs in the future. As mentioned earlier, the other schools were not going to sit idly by and watch Valdosta State rampage through the schedule without getting things going at their respective schools. Foster immediately changed the culture at Shorter, along with the nickname and uniforms. Colson's concerns that the journey through conference would not be easy this year proved to be true in every sense of the word.

The Rebels would find themselves behind the 8 ball during the latter stages of the conference season, having suffered three losses. All three losses occurred on the road: at LaGrange (54-51), Berry (56-54), and West Georgia (67-65).

Clearly, the conference coaches realized that they had to contain the Rebels' potent running game, forcing the game to become a defensive possession by possession half-court game. All three of these losses were close; a total of 7 points separated the Rebels from being undefeated. Losing tight, hotly contested, meaningful games might derail the championship aspirations of many teams, but not this group. The Rebel Spirit, which was part and parcel of their team DNA, was reflected in their ability to "get back up off the deck, regroup and refocus" thanks to their Floor Leadership (and you can pick any number of players who were influential in this regard, from Perry to Ritch to McCully to Johnson to Hodges, etc., down the line to freshmen like Ben Bates).

When West Georgia College rolled into Titletown with four games to go in the conference season, the Rebels were in trouble. They sat at 3-3, trailing both LaGrange and Shorter by a full game in the loss column (they were 4-2). The season was slipping away (a loss would mean certain elimination); it was time for the Rebels to draw a line in the sand and make their move. West Georgia had beaten the Rebels, 67-65, in Carrollton three weeks prior. Colson's Rebels responded with a record-breaking effort, blasting West Georgia, 116-74.

Opening jump ball vs. West Georgia.

The onslaught was led by Ritch with 31, Johnson with 18, Perry 15, McCully 13, Hodges and Bonovitch 8 each, who put the Rebels out in front early and then hit the accelerator! When they went to the bench with six minutes left, they were up 95-63. All the next group did was add 21 more points to the blowout. These were the guys Colson had said early in the season he was interested to see how they would adapt to the college game. Fike, McFarland, Mullins, Hearn, Strong, and Bates showcased their talent and Rebel Spirit by finishing the game playing through the echo of the whistle!

The game turned on the boards and defensive end. The Rebels overpowered the Braves on the boards, 53-31. The two 6-2 forwards (Ritch and Hodges) had 11 boards each. Bonovitch added another eight and McFarland seven in his limited minutes. The Rebels set a new VSC one-game scoring record with 116, which surpassed last season's 113 against Charleston.

Colson, though jubilant with the win, knew this win only kept the

Rebels within reach, saying "this victory over West Georgia keeps us in the race, but that's all. We have to get our feet back on the ground before we play Berry and Shorter again."

On Feb. 12, 1964, the Rebels faced Shorter in Rome, knowing another loss would spell the end to the title aspirations.

They had lost to Berry and needed to find a way to beat Foster's Shorter Hawks, who for the second season in a row had title aspirations of their own. This game would become a legend in its own right after the Rebels' powerful center, Chuck Bonovitch, came up lame with a blood blister on his foot and could not dress for the game. In Bonovitch's (6-5) place, Colson inserted 6-1 Tommy Johnson. Among the Rebels' starting five, no one was over 6-3, whereas Shorter had only one player under 6-3—everyone else was 6-5 to 6-7. What a display of relentless effort on the glass and on the defensive end! The Rebels' starting five played just about the entire game, scoring was balanced between the five, and Valdosta State never trailed, winning 56-53.

The win set up yet another Championship Playoff game between the Rebels and Shorter for the second-straight year. The game would be played in Columbus this year. Shorter did not want any part of a return trip to Macon—too many demons to deal with. On Feb. 28, the basketball gods were smiling on the Rebels again, who outlasted a Shorter slow-down game plan, 35-32. Colson said after the game that "we could play one another 99 times this year and neither team would ever win by more than three points." All three contests this year were determined by a total of seven points, and neither team sniffed 60 points.

Robert Maxwell described the low scoring affair as "a game which nearly drove the spectators into nervous hysteria and the radio audience to drink." He noted that the Rebels loved to run, but had shown they were willing to "hunker down" on the defensive end, especially after "the Gold Wave went into a freeze game for seven of the last 10 minutes of the game." Sammy Glassman wrote "the name of this game was defense and the stout hearted Rebels licked Shorter" at their own game.

Shorter's Foster decided to turn the game into a limited offensive game. One of Colson's gifts as a head coach is his ability to quickly determine what he felt worked and what did not, then adapt and adjust strategy accordingly. No game exemplifies this characteristic more than this one. Foster and Colson, who would become close friends over their careers, were playing chess, not checkers, in this game. Rather than overthink things or dwell on them and get locked up mentally, Colson was able to reframe the circumstance and make a call. After the game, Colson said "our game plan was to try to run on them, but they wanted to make it a defensive duel, so we adjusted and beat them playing their own game. This is a great bunch of men and they came through under tremendous pressure."

There were many moments to cherish in this game, none bigger than Preston Hodges' deflection and recovery of a Shorter jump shot with less than three minutes to play, breaking the Shorter stall strategy that began at the seven minute mark. After the deflection and recovery, McCully and Hodges took turns knocking down free throws to put the game away. There were not many possessions in this type of game, so defensive rebounding was especially crucial. The Rebels held a slight (but important) edge 21-17, Bonovitch had 6, Hodges and McCully 4 each. The remaining 7 rebounds were shared by the other players. Offensively, the Rebels were led by Bonovitch's 12 points, McCully 9, Ritch 6, Hodges 5, and Perry 3.

Colson acknowledged that while the Rebels "may have snuck in through the back door" they were again GIAC Champions, for the fourth year in a row. They had ascended into exceedingly rare air within team competition, a Four-Peat. While All-Conference Honors went to Bonovitch, Perry, and Ritch, the role, impact, and influence of every player on the roster cannot be stressed enough. Colson, who won Coach of the Year again, said "All the credit goes to my players." Colson had once again proven adept at taking a team of new players and returning lettermen in the fall, and developing them into a cohesive, unified team—the "me into us" mysterious process of team building.

The Georgia Southern Eagles were the Rebels' first-round opponent in the District 25 Tournament in Statesboro. The Eagles, under J.B.

Scearce, were a formidable opponent anywhere, but especially at home. Stetson played JU on the other side of the bracket.

The semifinal was a foul-plagued game from the beginning, with the Rebels accumulating a total of 28 fouls. The Eagles were called for 20 fouls and lost no one to five fouls. Georgia Southern was 35-for-41 from the charity stripe, contrasted to the Rebels' 15-for-23. The game turned in this particular area, as the Rebels could not overcome a 20-point deficit at the line, even though they shot the ball relatively effectively going 33-for-72 from the floor (46%). For the season, the Rebels shot 50%+ consistently.

The Rebels were down 54-36 at the half but clawed their way back into the contest at the 16:25 mark, outscoring the Eagles by 13 points and cutting their lead to 5 points. It was at that point that the dreaded Zebra effect took over, whistling fouls on Bonovitch and Hodges, sending them to the bench with five fouls each. From that point, it was an uphill battle as the Eagles' size inside created rebounds that led to fast breaks and more free throws. Post-game, Colson noted that "they had too much speed and made too many free throws." The Rebels were led in scoring by Ritch with 27, Perry and McCully had 16 each, and Tommy Johnson threw in 11. Bonovitch and Hodges scored 10 points total between them.

The 1963-64 season came to a crashing close in the first round of the District Tournament again, this time to the Eagles. Last year, it was JU. As the Rebels piled into the vans to go home, there were a couple of reflections going on in between their head and heart. First, they were now regulars in this postseason tournament, and second, by virtue of beating Georgetown (KY), they knew they could compete for this prized championship. Third, they were not accustomed to losing. Consequently, although there was a quiet tone on the way home, this bunch was very resilient and would begin circling next season's tournament—making it a target for them to work for and achieve.

Many of the players turned right around and headed for the baseball field: Mike Perry, Tommy Johnson, Dennis Fike, Bill Hearn, and Herman Hudson. As the spring sports wound to a close, the Annual Sports Awards Banquet was held. The award winners were:

- Ray McCully named Best Playmaker
- Tommy Johnson named Most Improved
- Bobby Ritch named MVP and Most Improved
- Mike Perry was the winner of the Rebel Spirit Award
- Mike Perry was named MVP in baseball
- Dennis Fike was named Most Outstanding Player in baseball
- Chuck Bonovitch was named to Who's Who in American Universities and Colleges

Perry spent four years under Colson. As he reflected on those years, he said "at the time we did not know or realize the enormity of what we accomplished or what it would mean to us in life. Now, 50 years later, it is clear that it was not an accident what we did or that so many have gone on to be successful in life and business. Coach Colson proved how important leadership is in any endeavor as he led us through those championship years. He was light years ahead of his time and this young man who some referred to as the 'boy from Dasher' would have a significant impact on basketball throughout the world. He created the tradition of championships at Valdosta State, which cannot be bought, but must be earned. When I arrived in 1960, we were just a little step above a club team. By the time I left, four years later, we had won a Four-Peat GIAC Championship.

How? Colson recruited hard-nosed guys that were resilient and would play through the echo of the whistle. Coach was creative, he and Coach Grant built the 'Shack' and made sure we had food to eat. More importantly, he brought discipline and teamwork into the lives of young men, teaching them how to trust one another to do their jobs every time. Everyone knew their role and did it beyond expectations. Not enough credit goes to the guys who did things other than scoring: setting the picks, snatching a rebound, throwing a great pass so the shooter could score. His concept of teamwork rubbed off on all of us, that everyone doing their job is critical. Through that experience, I learned how to have faith in the other guys. I gained respect for others and what their contributions would be. What a difference it made in my life, personally and professionally!"

Mike Perry

Mike finished his Rebel career having played in 77 games, scoring 1,127 points, and averaging 14.6. He is a member of the 1,000 Point club at Valdosta State and in the VSU Hall of Fame.

One of Coach Colson's enduring qualities as a leader and coach is that he would not dwell on things in the past; he would begin moving forward rather quickly. He would not wallow in the negative moments or circumstances. He would begin reaching out to peers such as Bennie Dees at ABAC, Pinholster at Oglethorpe, Joe Dean from Converse Shoes, and his old roommate, Jerry Jones for insights, recommendations, and thoughts about how to continue moving the Rebel basketball program forward. Ken Blanchard, noted leadership expert and author, describes this strategy as "+1" which means great leaders always ask themselves how they can get 1% or $1 or 1 FT % better next year. Blanchard says as a leader, you are either growing or dying. Colson has always been and will always be on the growth side, searching for the next +1. And this characteristic would make all the difference as Colson began his search for the next recruiting class!

6

⚜

1965-66: Oh so close!

1964-65: Taking the Next Step

Gary Colson was not one to remain fixated on the rearview mirror. He was all about reflecting and learning from losses, then moving on with what he had gleaned from that low moment in time. Although his record was a healthy 71-40 overall and a stellar 46-16 in the GIAC (with two unblemished, 12-0 seasons), he had not yet conquered the likes of Georgia Southern, Stetson, or JU—all formidable opponents. The winner of the District 25 Tournament went to Kansas City to play for a NAIA National Championship (the top 32 teams in the NAIA). While Colson and the Rebels were a dynasty in the making within the GIAC, they had another hilltop to climb—getting to KC.

Seeding in the District Tournament was critical. The number one seed hosted the tournament. The Dunkel Ratings were used for seeding purposes in many NAIA District Tournaments throughout the country in this era (including District 25, Florida-Georgia). Dick Dunkel, Sr. invented the Dunkel Ratings in New York in 1929 where he was a market researcher on Madison Avenue. He started with football then moved into basketball. Dunkel approached the NCAA and the NAIA, who jumped at the opportunity to have a neutral resource seed their district and national tournament.

Front row (L-R): Mike Terry, Ben Bates, Bobby Ritch, Letson Plant, Preston Hodges, Tommy Johnson. Second row: Gary Traylor, Ron Fortner, Paul Weitman, Paul Vick, Tommy MacFarland, Bob Lamphier, Dennis Fike. Third row: Ray McCully, Tommy Anderson, Head Coach Gary Colson, Jim Hunt, Bill Gillis

Dunkel's ratings assess relative strengths, based on the scoring margins of victory or loss and the quality of opposition. Dunkel's individual District Ratings were done by hand from index cards based on phone calls on Sunday with complete scores from within the district. He said, "we know at a glance how a team has done versus every other team in the district." The top-rated team in the district would host the tournament. For example, last season Georgia Southern was the one seed, JU the two seed, Stetson the three seed, and Valdosta State the four seed; therefore, Georgia Southern was the host.

Dunkel took notice of Colson and Valdosta State when they upset Georgetown (KY), for whom he had a high regard, along with the tight contests with FSU and JU. His personal notes to Colson were encouraging, pointing out that he expected to see the Rebels continue making positive strides toward Kansas City!

Colson was engaging, personable, and entertaining regardless of the circumstance. Although he was a fiery competitor who would fight for every inch in order to win, once the contest was over, the vivacious Colson personality took over and engaged foes as well as friends. He and Benny Dees, ABAC were peers and competitors for recruits yet talked frequently during and after the season, sharing thoughts on strategies as well as players. This is a primary reason the Rebels ended up with some incredible talent from ABAC over the years. Colson embraced and built a healthy relationship with Coach Pinholster from Oglethorpe. At this point in the journey to the top of the small college basketball world, Colson contacted his roommate from David Lipscomb, Jerry Jones, who was coaching in Indiana. Colson was quick to adapt and adjust to make another stride in a positive direction. In this case, he needed to continue to upgrade the depth of talent on the roster. In calling Jones, Colson hit a "vein of talent" unlike any he had found to date. Jones knew talent and character when he saw it is an understatement.

Indiana high school basketball players are legendary because it appears they are born into the world shooting and dribbling a basketball. Their basketball DNA and IQ in that era was considered the best in the world. Colson asked Jones to assist in locating and recruiting players with a high ceiling (tons of potential) the big schools might have overlooked, who had the character (Rebel Spirit) as well as the talent to play for the Rebels. These players had to be willing to work, to be coached, and develop their skills and systems understanding over time.

The Indiana pipeline was in operation quickly. Jones identified three players the Rebels should take: Ron Fortner, Bob Lamphier, and Mike Terry. Lamphier explained that "I had signed with Ball State prior to Jerry Jones calling me to discuss Valdosta State. When we went down to visit, we met the guys, saw the campus, etc. I decided I was headed south." These three would be the beginning of substantive recruiting on behalf of the Rebels by Jerry Jones, as well as a host of other family friends and associates.

I had never heard of Valdosta State when our head football coach caught me the hallway between classes explaining he had a letter for me. I looked at it and it had the Valdosta State logo on the envelope. Coach Colson had written to ask if I was interested. I found out the football coach, who had gone to college with Colson, had called him on my behalf. Then, before you know it, three of us are in the car with Coach Jones and his wife headed south. What an experience on that campus in the spring and listening to Coach Colson's recruiting. Next thing I knew, I was driving south with Ron Fortner in his '57 Chevy for one the great experiences in my life!

Mike Terry

In addition to these three quality freshmen, Colson snatched a highly regarded JC transfer from Miami Dade JC, Letson Plant. Other new additions this year were Paul Vick, Gary Traylor, and Paul Weitman, who Al Thornton characterized as a "bull in a china cabinet" when it came to rebounding. As Colson would say "fate was good to him," but a reminder that "luck is the residue of design."

Returning lettermen for the 1964-65 campaign were Ray McCully, Bobby Ritch, Preston Hodges, Tommy Johnson, Dennis Fike, Tommy MacFarland, and Ben Bates. Seven quality players; two All-Conference players in McCully and Ritch, four starters from the prior year, and an incredible 6th man, Ben Bates, who probably could have started at a number of other schools, and a post player with touch: 6-6, 220-pound Tommy MacFarland. The only challenge would be similar to previous seasons: There was no significant height and no real presence in the post. Yet this edition of the Rebels would prove that height is not necessarily the only key to winning championships. More importantly, the Rebel Spirit turns challenges into opportunities this year as in the past.

The starting lineup included 6-5 freshman Mike Terry, along with Ray McCully, Bobby Ritch, Preston Hodges, and Letson Plant. Tommy Johnson, Ben Bates, Paul Vick, Tommy MacFarland, and Paul Weitman played significant minutes off the bench. Although the core of the 1963-64 team was back, there were two new starters, Terry and Plant, which meant the Rebels would need some time to fine tune this offense before it became a well-oiled machine.

Bobby Ritch, Preston Hodges, Tommy Johnson, Dennis Fike, Tommy MacFarland, and Ben Bates with Coach Colson

The Rebels went into the Christmas break with a 4-2 record, losing only to FSU in Tallahassee and at Georgia Southern. Returning from Christmas and right before the conference schedule, the Rebels would face another rival, Oglethorpe. Although Colson and Pinholster were good friends off the court, their competitive spirits showed when they hit the court. The Rebels had never beaten the Stormy Petrels in 10 tries. Colson told Sammy Glassman he was bringing the team back early so they could get "plenty of extra practice to get ready to play the 6-3 Petrels."

Oglethorpe's lineup featured a front line of 6-7, 6-6 and 6-4, with the guards standing in at 5-11 and 6-3. The Rebels countered with 5-10, 6-2, 6-2, 6-4, and 6-5. They were decidedly shorter in stature, but not heart! Al Thornton, a Valdosta State fan from the day Colson took over, describes this group as "playing their hearts out every time they went onto the floor. They were a family; you could see they cared about one another and played that way. Other teams might have more talent or be bigger, but they could not match the heart of the Rebels!" That relentless, resilient Rebel Spirit would never let up or give in. No matter

Letson Plant scores against Lagrange

what the odds or circumstances, they were going to play through the echo of the whistle!

On this January evening in Titletown, the Rebels began taking the next step toward a District Championship as they knocked off the Oglethorpe Stormy Petrels for the first time in history, 65-53. At this point in the season, Ritch was averaging 16.8 ppg, Plant 13.8 ppg, and Terry 12 ppg.

In mid-January, the Rebels faced off with the Seahawks from UNC Wilmington. Again, the Rebels were decidedly shorter than their tall and talented opponents; nevertheless, the Rebels found a way to pull this game out of the fire in the last 14 minutes of the game, after trailing by 14 points.

The cliff-hanger of the contest went down to the last five seconds with the score tied at 60. Plant hooked up with Ritch with a long pass, after which Ritch drove the ball to the rim for the layup and victory with a fractional second left on the clock! Anyone who had watched the Rebels knew Ritch was the guy who was going to get the ball, and a herd of wild animals could not stop him from getting to the ball and making a play. Thornton acknowledged that "Everyone knew Bobby was the go-to guy when the Rebels had to have a bucket." Bobby says he learned to "accept that responsibility from my high school coach, Garney Hatch. I had a lot of confidence in my ability to get the shot off and make it. That's all due to the work Coach Hatch put in with me at High Springs."

Plant scored 22 points, Terry 15, and Ritch 12. The Rebels got handled on the glass 30-23, which led to put backs for the Seahawks, who outshot the Rebels from the floor 51% to 41%. Ritch, Plant, and Johnson were the rebound leaders for the Rebels. At this point in the season, the Rebels' record stood at 6-2, with the conference schedule dead ahead. The lack of inside presence would continue to raise its ugly head as the season progressed from here.

The GIAC would come down to the Shorter rivalry for the fourth-straight year. Bill Foster's Hawks were tall, talented, and hungry. More than likely, Foster reminded his team that Summerford said, "Shorter is always a bridesmaid, never a bride" at the conclusion of one of the previous playoff games between the two rivals. The Rebels maintained serve in Valdosta, 74-63 and lost in Rome, leaving both teams sitting atop the standings with identical 9-1 conference records. Consequently, there was a playoff game between the two teams for the third-straight year to determine the GIAC Champion. The game would be played in Titletown, which meant Foster's nemesis, PA announcer Red Cross, would get another opportunity to charge up Rebel Nation! Foster told Colson that Cross' energy and style was worth 10 points, getting the crowd riled up into a state of frenzy.

Not often did the Rebels lose at home to conference foes; they had dispatched Shorter earlier in the year. On this cold night late in February, the lack of interior size was a difference, as Foster's charges dominated the Rebels in the paint and on the boards. Jimmy Chastain, a 6-5 talent from South Carolina, scored 22 points and collected 16 rebounds, a double-double. The 16 rebounds were more than the Rebels had in total. Scoring totals for the Rebels were McCully 15, Ritch 12, Terry and Jonson 8 each, Plant 7, Vick 4, Fortner 2, and Weitman 1. The Hawks celebrated on the Rebels' home floor, Foster telling the Atlanta Constitution that this victory was the "finest of the season and even tastes better than going undefeated!"

The Rebels would play 20 games in 1964-65 and go 16-4 overall, and 9-1 in the GIAC. McCully, Ritch, and Plant were GIAC All-Conference players. Ritch added the Atlanta Journal first Team All-State to his list of postseason honors. The AJC called Ritch "maybe the best player on this All Star squad." Quite a compliment coming from the AJC since there were two Georgia Tech players, one from Georgia and a highly thought of guard from Georgia Southern on the first team. Ritch had earned every honor he received in his three years. Leading the Rebels scoring attack this year,

Vick (25), Terry (30), and Ritch (44) during the Oglethorpe game.

Ritch finished the campaign averaging 18.2 ppg, while Plant finished with 13.3 ppg.

Although the loss to Shorter was still stinging everyone's heart and mind, there was much to celebrate, especially the first victory over rival Oglethorpe.

There is no question in athletics that some losses hurt worse than others, and the loss at home to Shorter in a playoff game stung! And would retain its sting in the hearts and minds of every Rebel for the next six months.

The winners of the awards in basketball are pictured at the left along with Coach Colson. From the left: Ben Bates, Paul Weitman, Coach Colson, Letson Plant, Bobby Ritch, and Ray McCully.

In great learning cultures, such moments as the loss to Shorter are a great opportunity for reflection, which is a major aspect of the learning process. The reflection process is as simple as these three questions (in Organizational Development they are known as Stop, Start, and Continue):

- What worked, and needs to continue?
- What did not work, and needs to be stopped?
- What needs to be started?

It was clear to Colson that his offense was productive. He had talented players and had built a championship culture based on the Rebel Spirit. What stalled the Rebel Championship train this season was a lack of an inside presence. We mentioned earlier in the book Colson was not one to wallow in guilt and shame of defeat. He would get up and dust his britches off and get about fixing things. In this case, he needed some height to go with his talented, resilient, and relentless warriors. He did not have to go far to find the right guy! He called Benny Dees at ABAC in Tifton, Georgia, who had someone who checked off all of the prerequisites for the job and who would become the Monster in the Middle for the Rebels!

1965-66: The Return to Glory!

For four-straight years, Bill Foster's Shorter Hawks had become the chief rival within the GIAC, fighting the Rebels to a draw during the regular season and forcing four-straight playoff games. Colson and Foster were playing chess, not checkers. Colson would make a strategic move; Foster would counter. Both were passionate lifelong learners who continued to learn from others in order to get an edge. Both were very self-aware, acknowledging their strengths and making every effort to become aware of their limitations and areas to improve in. Just as in chess, Colson had to make the next move, in this case someone who could dominate the middle.

Bennie Dees was a great friend and loyal supporter of Colson. ABAC had a 6-6 horse, Gwendell McSwain. When I say "horse," consider the physical attributes: 6-6, 215 lean pounds, with close to a seven foot wingspan. Then add his agility, his ability to move side to side easily, and finally, he had at least a 30-inch vertical. That is the equivalent of someone 6-10 who can defend away from the paint as well as control the paint. Secondly, and most importantly, McSwain was as intense a competitor as could be found. You never had to wonder if he was bringing the full load with him on either end of the floor or the game. Simply put, he was the "Monster of the Middle" Colson was looking for.

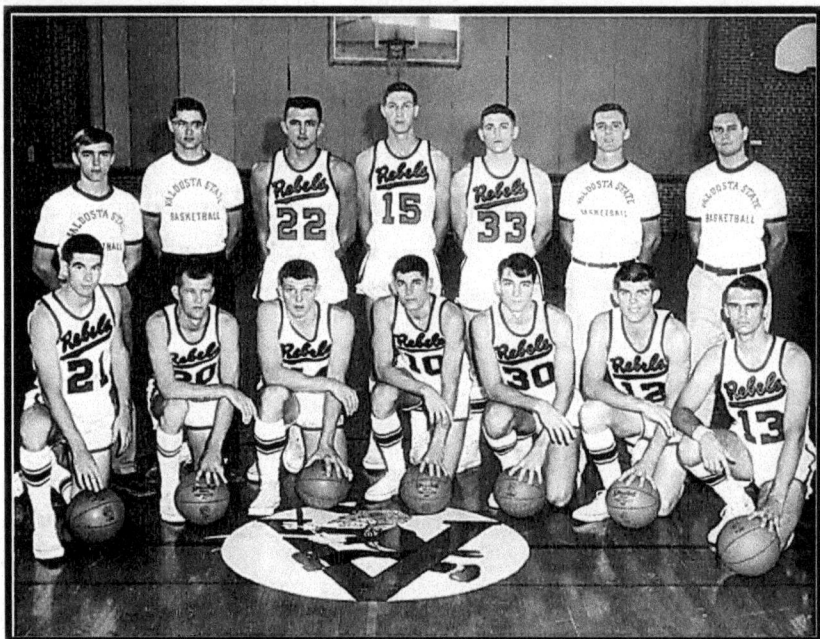

Front Row, left to right: Tommy Johnson, Ray McCully, Bobby Ritch, Ben Bates, Mike Terry, Bob Lamphier, and Ron Fortner. Second Row: Robert. Deloach (Mgr.), Gene Deariso (Mgr.), Letson Plant, Gwendell McSwain, Paul Weitman, Head Coach Gary Colson, and Mike Summerford (Assistant Coach).

This is how Al Thornton describes McSwain: "Goose was a good ole country boy, humble and he was going to get the job done. I saw him in high school, at ABAC and then with the Rebels. He was as tough as they came—would play right through injuries. He poured his entire heart and soul into every possession, rebound, and game on both ends! He was willing to set teeth-rattling picks, to tipping the ball multiple times until only he could claim the rebound, come off his man to help by deflecting a shot or pass—100% unselfish!" Simply, Goose "Mac" came equipped with the Rebel Spirit from the outset. Colson said as much to Hal Ratcliff, "He could mean the difference between going to Kansas City to play for a National Championship or staying home and watching TV. His greatest asset is his ability to control the backboards and get our fast break going by hitting the outlet in a hurry."

The anticipation for the upcoming 1965-66 season brought elevated expectations the Rebels would get back on the GIAC Championship train and take the next step toward KC. The reasons were:

- McSwain was the only addition to the squad loaded with experience.
- McCully, Ritch, Plant, Johnson, and Weitman were returning Seniors.
- Bates (Jr.), Terry, Lamphier, and Fortner (Sophomores) returned after a year where all three were contributors.
- McCully, Ritch, and Plant were All Conference. Ritch had been identified by the AJC as maybe the best player in Georgia last season.
- This bunch of competitors would do what they had the entirety of their careers—demonstrate an incredible level of resilience by getting back up after being knocked down by Shorter and bring the fight to them this season.
- Lastly, new uniforms reflecting the NBA 76ers style were bound to have a positive effect (per Mike Perry).

This season, the Rebels' starters looked like this: McCully (5-10) – 6.7 ppg, Ritch (6-2) – 18.3 ppg, Plant (6-4) – 13.3 ppg, Terry (6-5) – 12.8 ppg, and Weitman (6-3) – 2.6 ppg/McSwain (6-6). With this starting group, the Rebels could walk onto the floor anytime, against anybody, anywhere, and not have to worry about being overwhelmed by size or physicality. This group was as talented skill-wise as any, their collective basketball IQ was off the charts, and they were committed team players to the man. They reflected the absolute best of the Rebel Spirit; they were relentless and resilient warriors!

While Ritch was well known and targeted defensively by every opponent in an attempt to limit his touches and shots, this season proved that would be a flawed strategy. Letson Plant served notice last season he could light up the scoreboard. The head coach shared his expectations and perspective of Plant's potential. "Plant has the potential to be as good as Bobby, maybe better, if he could be more consistent. If he plays to his potential, then we're headed to KC." Plant was an athletic guard from Miami Dade CC, where he was used to running and gunning. Miami Dade perennially led the nation's JUCOs in scoring, averaging 110 ppg. He and Ritch faced off as seniors in Florida and had a healthy respect for one another. Ritch helped Plant assimilate into the Wheel offensive system last season, which was more methodical than the fast break oriented club he played for in South Florida. Moreover, Plant could score, play defense, and rebound with anyone. Plant adjusted to defending smaller guards, especially because of his length and jumping ability. He said, "I like to stuff them early in the game, it makes them gun shy the rest of the night." His role this year cannot be understated!

In addition to Ritch and Plant, the Rebels would look to Mike Terry, who started since he was a freshman. He was 6-5, which made him the tallest man on last year's team. He understood the game and had the requisite skills to make a difference on both ends. Marty Lehmann, who would arrive Terry's senior year, said, "Mike was an incredible scorer who could shoot the jumper but take the ball into the teeth of the defense and somehow get the shot off and get fouled. The bucket would count, and he would invariably head to the FT line. He could make the most unorthodox shots look easy and make them." Mike was a competitor who fought for every inch of real estate in the paint on rebounds, was willing to share the ball on offense, and set picks to spring others—in other words, he fit right into Colson's system. He was the third leading scorer off last year's team, along with tying Ritch for the most rebounds with 134, and by all rights should have been All Conference.

The bench would be as important as the starters. Look at this list of players coming off the bench:

- Ben Bates, arguably one of the greatest 6th men in the history of

Rebel basketball, just a sophomore, who won the coveted Rebel Spirit Award last season

- Tommy Johnson, a senior, who made major contributions in major wins over his first three years
- Ron Fortner, a 6-2 sophomore guard, who made significant contributions as a freshman
- Paul Weitman, a 6-3, 235-pound bull in the paint and on the glass

For Floor Leadership, he had two great captains, Ray McCully, and Bobby Ritch. Both had been with Colson for three seasons and knew what the head coach was looking for and were fierce competitors. The players selected these two warriors and leaders as their captains!

The head coach said, "the team made an excellent choice, both are capable leaders and well respected—looked up to by every one of their teammates!" Colson was well aware he had arguably the best guard tandem in Georgia between McCully and Ritch, and maybe in the Southeast. When you combine their athletic abilities, skills, and leadership impact, as a head coach you are thinking much bigger than the GIAC Championship, maybe winning it all in KC.

Colson knew he had senior leadership in McCully, who operated as the floor general. Ritch confirmed Colson's confidence, saying "Ray was as cool as the other side of the pillow. He saw the entire floor; he anticipated what was going to happen and got the ball to the scorers. Literally, he was the 'Little General' because he was in control of what was going on. Ray was such a great passer, who could put the right speed and location on every pass." Al Thornton, a devoted lifelong Rebel fan, describes McCully as the "sparkplug of the team, the glue, the catalyst! When Ray hit the locker room and gym, there was no messing around. He was a serious and fiery competitor to be so mild mannered off the court." Colson referred to McCully as the guy "who has made our offense click for the last three seasons. He's the kind of player who holds everything together." McCully started as a freshman (was the Rebels MVP), was All Conference and District 25 All Tournament as a sophomore and junior. It is important to note that while Ray was ready to reclaim the championship and move forward toward KC, he was torn whether to play or not. Beyond basketball, he was trying to balance life with a new baby, work, and class. Ray shared that the decision to play was made in "October just before the season tipped off." As Colson says, "fate was looking after the Rebels," McCully suited up and was ready to go!

What more could be said about Ritch than what has been written already. Anytime the AJC says you are potentially the best backcourt player in the state, that is a big statement! But Ritch's stats and honors back it up—as they say, "the proof is in the pudding!" Last season, Bobby was All GIAC, AJC First Team All-State, NAIA Honorable Mention AA, team MVP, and the leading scorer and rebounder for the Rebels the last two years. He was as impactful on the defensive end as he was on the offensive end, always taking the toughest offensive player the opponent had (and putting a glove on them). He made the steal and breakaway layup to beat Shorter in Macon his freshman year.

Coach Colson was optimistic, not to the point of publicly licking his chops, but by describing his level of expectation to Sammy Glassman before the season: "We have an experienced team and high hopes! On the other hand, the schedule is the most ambitious we've tackled."

The 30 game schedule shaped up in the following manner:

- The non-conference schedule included FSU (one game), Georgia Southern (one game), Tampa (two), Oglethorpe (two), and JU (two). All of these teams were considered upper echelon in competition, so if the Rebels could clear these hurdles, then they could find their way to KC.

Ray McCully, and Bobby Ritch with Coach Colson

The conference schedule would not begin until mid-January with Shorter and Piedmont at home, then the Shorter–Berry trip to Rome the following weekend. Shorter would be the big challenge again this year. It is time to tip off this season, here are the highlights.

- After going 3-0 in the first week, the Rebels rolled into Tully Gymnasium to face a strong FSU squad. The 'Noles eked out a 69-68 win when their stud, Gary Shull, drove for layup and was fouled (controversial call) by McSwain at the rim. The game was back and forth throughout, with neither team managing to gain leverage until the 3-point play at the end of the game. Ritch was unstoppable—FSU tried numerous defenders and strategies, none of which worked. Ritch went 17-for-25 from the floor and added 2-for-4 FTs for 36 points. One of the great performances in Rebel history, considering the opponent and the location, at their house! But the game was more than the Ritch show. It was as impressive defensive effort as the Rebels delivered. Coach Colson told Sammy Glassman after the game, "Our defensive effort was the best a VSC team has ever played since I've been here!" The taller Seminoles bested the Rebels on the glass by a single rebound. Weitman and McSwain led the assault on the glass, followed by Terry, Johnson, and Ritch. McCully made life miserable for the FSU backcourt by bird dogging every pass, making three critical interceptions in the second half which led to buckets. McSwain limited Shull to one FG in the first half. Shull ended up with 19 points for the night, three of them on the play at the end of the game. The game turned at the FT line. FSU went 11-for-14, whereas the Rebels slipped, going 8-for-14. If .... there was not time to cry about "spilled milk" since Dana Kirk's powerful Spartans from Tampa were on tap two days later.

- The Rebels would steamroll Tampa in Valdosta and turn around to face JU's Dolphins in historic Swisher Gym two nights later. This was a strong JU squad under the direction of Joe Williams, who took over last year, and who would lead the Dolphins to the NCAA title game vs. UCLA in four years. JU had left the NAIA for greener pastures and the notoriety of the NCAA (as did Stetson and Florida Southern). The Rebels lost in OT to the Dolphins. The Rebels returned home to win the next six games before their last pre-conference tussle with rival and powerful Georgia Southern. The Eagles escaped with a narrow victory to leave the Rebels with an overall record of 10-3.

- The GIAC schedule opened with victories over Shorter and a blowout of Piedmont, 100-42. The Rebels were off and running, racing down the conference tracks to an 8-1 record with a date with West Georgia in Valdosta—the only thing standing in their way to a fifth GIAC Championship in six years. The capstone game was never close, as the Rebels laid the wood to the Braves,

99-51. Although West Georgia attempted to play stall ball, the Rebel's intense defensive pressure led to a 41-14 halftime lead, after which the onslaught by the Rebel bench continued to pound the hapless crew from Carrollton. Ritch put up 24 points, Lamphier 17, McSwain 13, Fortner and Weitman 10 points. McSwain had 13 boards, followed by Ritch and Weitman with 8 each. Not one West Georgia player reached double figures. The Rebels were once again GIAC Champions!

- In the midst of the second half of the season, the Rebels had five non-conference games: Two vs. Oglethorpe, one each vs. JU, Tampa, and St. Leo. Earlier in the season they had lost to JU in OT by 1, at FSU by 1, routed Tampa by 20 in Valdosta, and lost to Georgia Southern by 4. JU paid the return visit to Valdosta, where the Rebels handled them easily by 15 points in front of a rabid, boisterous Rebel nation crowd. Next up was the trip to Tampa, which was a tough win accomplished against officiating and Dana Kirk's antics from the sideline. Those who made the trips know what it's like to go down to play Dana Kirk's Spartans, knowing the calls would not go our way. It was a difficult place to play and win, nonetheless, on this night, the Rebels were the toughest team in Tampa Bay. Then St. Leo was pounded into the floor of the gym at "Winnerville" before the District 25 Tournament started. That left the two-game set against bitter rival, Oglethorpe. The Rebels paid a visit to Pinholster's talented squad in Atlanta, where they manhandled Oglethorpe 82-56, during which Pinholster would be seen throwing chairs and telling the press, "they just gutted us!"

- The dominance carried over to Oglethorpe's trip in Valdosta, where the Rebels duplicated the blowout. The Rebels were ready and went to work early, sprinting out to an 8-0 lead, from which they never looked back. They only hit the gas pedal and blew them out! Ritch scored 25, going 10-for-19 from the floor. McSwain got the double-double with 22 points and 16 boards, and Plant added 17.

Bates and Weitman fight for a rebound

- The Rebels swept Oglethorpe for the first time in history and passed a major mile marker on the road to the District 25 title. The Rebels ended the season at 24-4 and 9-1 in the GIAC, with a 5th GIAC Championship and trip to the District 25 tournament. The opponent would be Georgia Southern with their 6-10 All American, Bill Pickens, standing in the way. J.B. Scearce's Eagles were highly ranked, for good reason—they were talented and deep. They had had their way with the upstart Rebels since

Colson arrived. The Rebels had vanquished the other District 25 rivals JU and Tampa, as well as rival Oglethorpe; all that was necessary was this landmark victory.

The Eagles would come into the Rebels' gym for the first ever District 25 Tournament hosted by Valdosta State. The atmosphere was rocking side-to-side pandemonium with a standing room only crowd! The Rebel Nation made their presence known and felt by the Eagles. Wilbert Harrison's "Going to Kansas City" was blaring 60 minutes before the tip!

The game was as a championship heavyweight fight should be: blow for blow, no quarter, and onto the next play. The game was tight, with neither team able to gain leverage; until late in the game with minutes remaining, a loose ball rolled toward the sideline and Ritch made his typical Kamikaze effort to retrieve the ball along with a Georgia Southern player, who was matching him effort for effort. There was a collision in advance of either player touching the ball, a whistle and Ritch had made his last play for the Rebels.

After Ritch left with five fouls, the Eagles shot FTs and had the leverage to finish the game on top. Ritch recalls the play vividly, as well as the conversation with the official after the game. "Both of us made an incredible effort to get to the ball and we collided. The official who made the call, whom I knew, came up to me after the game and said he had made a mistake—the play was a no call." With that, the sounds of Wilbert Harrison's "Going to Kansas City" would not be heard until the Rebels returned to the floor next year.

To provide some context to the year and especially credit to Georgia Southern, they played in the Finals at KC—getting blasted by the eventual winner; but the Eagles won four out of five in KC, which is not easy. They were good, not great though. The Rebels lost five games by a total of less than 10 points. That is how close they were to the promised land. Close does not cut it in these circumstances, the 1965-'66 edition of the Rebels finished 24-5, the 2nd most wins in school history but just a fingertip short of their objective—a trip to KC!

Reflections are important after every season, but especially with these seniors who contributed so much over the last four years: Ray Mc-Cully, Bobby Ritch, Dennis Fike, and Tommy Johnson. What did this group accomplish?

- They won three GIAC Championships in four years.
- Their overall record was 69-23 and 33-7 in the GIAC.
- They left having beaten Oglethorpe two times within the same season, splitting the season series with JU, beaten highly ranked Georgetown, and having scared the beans out of FSU (twice), losing by a total of 3 points. They had lifted the Rebel profile from South Georgia obscurity to a national presence. Don Dunkel wrote Colson after the FSU games explaining either of these games would have been one the greatest upsets in the history of the game, and he expected to see the Rebels continuing to make the move toward the coveted trip to KC.
- Bates, Devivo, Fike, Fortner, Johnson, Lamphier, and Perry (he was eligible to play baseball) rolled right into baseball and won the Rebels' first GIAC Championship.
- Fortner, Deariso, and Plant ran Cross Country and won the GIAC Cross Country Championship.
- Fike, Johnson, McCully, and Ritch were inducted into the Valdosta State Athletic HOF.

Fike and Johnson were incredible players who came off the bench whenever called and carried on without a hitch. Both were stalwarts on the diamond, with Johnson winning an MVP during his career. These guys were leaders in their own right, regardless of whether they started or came off the bench. One of the key reasons the Rebels were considered the most relentless of the relentless was that players like Johnson and Fike were as tenacious and relentless as the starters. There was not going to be a respite for the opponents and if they were thinking that they received a rude awakening; these guys could play and execute at high levels. Bench Leadership falls on every man who is sitting on the bench and these players set a tone by the effort they put forth every day in practice and every second they spent on the floor. The Rebels were tough because their depth from a Rebel Spirit perspective was unmatched by any other team, including FSU. A tip of the hat to these players, who often go unsung!

GIAC Champions

1960-61
1961-62
1962-63
1963-64
1965-66

Bobby Ritch, whom Norm Sloan (UF Basketball Coach) described as "too small to play in the SEC", would continue to receive postseason accolades. Ritch was the leading scorer in the GIAC for three years, a three-time GIAC All-Conference selection, GIAC MVP this season, Honorable Mention All American last season, District 25 MVP this year, AJC All State last year, and Second Team All American this year. In his career, Ritch played in 93 games, averaging 18.1 points per game in a team-oriented offense (of which he was willing to hit the open man rather than forcing a shot), and scored 1,684 points (fourth on the Valdosta State All Time list within the 1,000 point club). Sloan's assessment only measures the physical stature of a player, not his character or heart or head (basketball IQ). Bobby Ritch's competitive desire was ferocious, fueling his work ethic – which only sharpened his skills. As Colson said, fate smiled on the Rebels when Studdard called four years ago to set up a tryout with a kid from High Springs—the rest is history.

Ray McCully showed up the same time as Ritch, and wow what a tandem they were! McCully was as cool on the surface point guard as any coach could ever want, while a volcanic competitive spirit raged below. Ray was from Kentucky, where many say the sport was invented—not in Indiana. He started four years in high school, then played in the Marines for four years during his enlistment. When he fell into Colson's lap, he had played serious amounts of basketball at high levels of competition, since military ball included many players who had played in college before enlistment. McCully started all four years for Colson and, looking through the record book, there is not another point guard who did that for Colson at Valdosta State. Colson said, "Ray's the glue, he keeps things in order and under control." Al Thornton said when "Ray walked into the locker room or onto the floor, the tone got intense and focused, there was no horseplay; and he did not have to say a word!" McCully was MVP his first year, All GIAC, and All District 25 during his career. Coaches at every level say the first thing they need is a quarterback that is stone cold focused, determined, unselfish—willing to do the dirty little tasks, recognizing and capitalizing on opportunities, resilient—knowing how to get on to the next play, etc. McCully checks all those boxes and more!

Colson wrapped up his comments about the Dynamic Duo, saying "they've been with me four years and they know what I want to do before I do! They complement one another, McCully feeds Ritch, while Bobby has the instincts to be in the right place at the right time. Ritch is at his best when McCully is on the floor."

Jim Collins says great leaders are those who have extremely high levels of humility and determination, which he labels as Level 5 leaders. Collins says Level 5 leaders display a powerful mixture of personal humility and indomitable will (relentless and resilient), they are incredi-

bly ambitious, but their ambition is first and foremost for the cause, for the organization and its purpose, not themselves. The four men graduating (Fike, Johnson, McCully, and Ritch) definitely fit Collins' description of Level 5 leaders. Coach Colson had men who represented the Rebel Spirit every day, in every way, in every circumstance. That is why the Rebels compete with any team, anytime, anywhere!

McCully reminisced about his four years at Valdosta State under Colson. "Coach Colson kept the commitments he made to me, recruited exceptional players, and made sure there was intense competition at practice for playing time—we pushed one another hard. He made sure we were prepared for each opponent and had us believing we could compete with anyone. I went there looking for an education and a chance to play ball and walked away with the fringe benefit of lifetime friendships with my teammates."

Ray McCully and Bobby Ritch

Ritch reflected on his four years, explaining that "he had had the opportunity to leave and did not accept it, and I have been grateful ever since. I have lifetime friendships from those four years that no amount of money can buy. I am grateful to Jim Nichols, for what he brought to the young, upstart program in the beginning, as well as the military veterans who played—Angie, Ray, Chuck, etc. I was 17 when I arrived, and their mature leadership had a profound effect on me and the younger players. The veterans understood what it meant to play for one another and the program, since they had been through military training. Consequently, we had a level of maturity as a team many teams do not ever find. And we were never intimidated by any team or player! There's volumes of stories that continue today, because those four years have never ended since we are best friends and continue to see and talk to one another regularly."

Tommy Johnson offered this reflection: "I graduated from Valdosta HS and did not have clear direction. Coach Colson and Coach Grant showed up, offered me an opportunity to play both basketball and baseball. They put an amazing group of men together that became a 'brotherhood' of sorts, all the way down to pooling their meager funds to buy and share a beat-up car for transportation. We literally became brothers since we were together 24 hours a day. We cared about one another then, as well as today. We learned to set aside our ego and put the team first, the discipline necessary to run Colson's Wheel offense, and the heart and tenacity required to play stiff defense. There's no way to put a price tag on the impact it had on my life professionally and personally. Today, 50 years later, we are still brothers! Priceless!"

Consequently, it was no wonder Colson was named NAIA Regional Coach of the Year, as well as the GIAC Coach of the Year. In eight years, Colson had moved the needle from a startup club team to a program with a national profile and wherewithal to play anyone, anytime, anywhere. His overall record stood at an amazing 137-52, with 24 of those losses coming in the first two years. Sammy Glassman noted that "he's regarded as one of the top young hoop mentors in the country, regardless of league or location." Glassman also wrote that Colson is "recognized as one of Valdosta's top amateur tennis players" which only highlights Colson's insatiable competitive drive and desire, as well as his athleticism and skill. (Colson led the VSC Tennis Team to their first GIAC Championship the previous season.) Colson had high octane enthusiasm, a relentless competitive streak, and was extremely resilient—recovering, learning, adapting, and regaining his balance and bearings quickly in the face of any adversity. Most importantly, he recognized talent and character when he saw it, and was able to recruit effectively through his friendly nature, and his enthusiasm and optimism. Tommy Johnson said, "we took on the mindset of our two leaders, Colson and Grant, along with the attitude from leaders in the locker room, and never looked back."

McSwain goes for a rebound.

The end-of-season assessment was the Rebels bounced back to win the GIAC a fifth time in six years, and continued making inroads toward winning the District 25 postseason tournament, coming up just short vs. Georgia Southern, a team who made it to the finals of the NAIA National Championship. Perry and McCully both agreed that "every year, we got a little better. Colson elevated the talent and enhanced the depth." Ritch continued, saying "we just kept building on the championship tradition that those who had come before us built against very difficult schedules."

While lamenting the loss of the Rebel version of the four horseman (McCully, Ritch, Johnson, and Fike) Colson was somewhat optimistic because he had five talented players returning: McSwain in the middle, Lamphier and Terry on the wings, Fortner running the point, and Bates as the 6th man extraordinaire. In addition, he had Danny Petrovich coming off the freshman team. In his opinion, he needed only 1-2 players to put the Rebels over the top and headed to KC in March 1967. Again, fate was smiling on Colson and the Rebels as spring turned to summer in '66; he would be the recipient of a major recruiting coup in the Southeast.

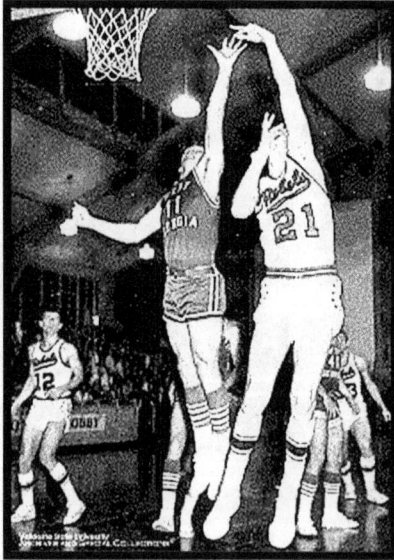

Tommy Johnson scores against West Georgia

7

$\circledast$

1966-68 Bound and Determined to Get to Kansas City

Gene "Syrup" Deariso was the Student Manager for the Rebels from 1965-67. He was beloved by the coaches, staff, and players. His nickname came from his distinctive dialect, which was slowest Southern drawl anyone ever heard. Marty Lehmann (1967-'71) shares "my Dad and I traveled from Gary, Indiana to Valdosta for a tryout. We slept in the basement of the gym on bunk beds. This guy named Syrup showed up on Saturday morning around 7 a.m. speaking a foreign language we could not decipher. We got up and followed him to breakfast where we were able to translate his dialect and messages. It was the thickest Southern drawl I would ever hear to this day; it was so slow and thick you could cut it with a knife." It was Syrup's job to make sure Wilber Harrison's "Going to Kansas City" and Duane Eddy's "Rebel Rouser" were playing at every practice, before games, etc., to remind everyone what was at stake. Another role of his was to sit in the front seat of the Green Hornet and control the radio stations. Syrup knew the radio dial like the back of his hand and ensured the Rebels' travel included the hottest songs of the day on the top stations around the Southeast and country (especially when returning at night, when the signals of most stations were inaccessible on the road, he could locate WOWO or WLS or WSB without any problems). Suffice it to say he left memorable and lasting impressions on all us, because every time we hear Harrison's "Going to Kansas City" we have two thoughts, going to KC and Syrup. He made sure it was imprinted on everyone's heart and head as the Rebels got ready to open camp in the fall of '66.

Gene "Syrup" Dearsio

Gary Colson had proved beyond a shadow of a doubt he could creatively resolve the narrow funding boundaries (others refer to this as a wing and a prayer) that impacted recruiting and scholarship numbers. As mentioned earlier, he and Coach Grant had repurposed the old Tiger Stadium Offices into an athletic dorm called the "Shack." The coaches could offer players (especially those that could play both basketball and baseball) Room scholarships in addition to tuition. Then they located restaurants that would feed the players (Board). This is the strategy they used to overcome the funding challenges through 1965 and another reason player after player stated that Colson "looked after them and was loyal to them." Then, fates were smiling on Colson again as an old friend of Dr. Thaxton asked if his son might be considered for a scholarship.

Although Dr. Thaxton was a huge fan and proponent of the Rebels, he literally had no idea how many scholarships the Rebels had or what they contained. His management style provided that the Controller, Shealy McCoy (who was tight fisted with funds), controlled operations through the funding of budgets. Mike Perry and Gary Bass (Athletic Committee Faculty Chairman) describe the scholarships as "the $30 Chamber of Commerce scholarship." That gives you an idea of the fiscal constraints the coaches faced up to this moment in time.

Dr. Thaxton had worked on his Ph.D. at the University of Indiana, where he had become close friends with a minister in the area. He called Dr. Thaxton (they had kept in close touch over the years) to ask if his son could get a tryout. Dr. Thaxton approached Gary Bass, inquiring about the possibility of a scholarship for his friend's son. Bass, a huge Rebels fan, Colson advocate, and friend, explained there were no funds available and that the coaches literally had to squeeze nickels out of pennies to get players here. As the conversation wound down, Dr. Thaxton looked at Bass and said, "I will take care of that immediately." Whatever conversation was had between the President and the Comptroller, the scholarship funding riddle was resolved, and the Rebels had a full complement of scholarships moving forward.

Consequently, Colson had enough scholarship money to create a freshman team. The Frosh would play other freshman teams, JUCOs, etc. A player off of last season's Freshman Team who would see action this year was Danny Petrovich. To reload the Frosh unit, Colson brought in players such as John Trimnell, Paul O'Brien, Dale Croft, Tommy Morrell, Robert McKinney, Gary Voorhees, Gary Vaught, and a couple of walk-ons. McKinney was 6-10, the tallest player in Valdosta State history at the time. The Frosh team was Colson's strategy to reload instead of rebuilding every couple of years, and he needed someone he could trust to develop the players, the culture, as well as the offensive and defensive systems used by the Rebels.

Jim Melvin, who had played for Colson and quarterbacked his first

GIAC Championship squad (undefeated), had completed his Master's at UGA and was ready to return home ("Valdosta is where I wanted to coach"). Coach Melvin had left Valdosta and coached high school ball before heading to UGA, where he served as an assistant coach for the UGA Freshman. In Melvin, Colson got the perfect complement to his coaching and management style, someone who knew the offensive and defensive systems inside and out, and someone who thoroughly understood what the Rebel Spirit and culture were all about. More importantly, Jim Melvin was a motivator of men, a great teacher, and added another layer of creativity and imagination to the head coach's cupboard. As a bonus, he brought along an unbelievable recruiting coup at the time, Bryan Phillips.

1966-67 Freshman Team

Colson only needed one or two pieces for the 1966-67 club to make it a legitimate National Championship contender. Before Jim Melvin left Athens for Valdosta, he called Colson to let him know Bryan Phillips was leaving UGA, and would he want to talk to the 6-6, 250-pound forward that could shoot the lights out from 20 feet, was fast enough to be invited to the Atlanta Falcons camp to try out for tight end, and was an aggressive bull in the paint? Needless to say, Bigun' checked all of Colson's boxes and moved from Athens to Valdosta. In the space of two seasons, UGA had let McSwain and Phillips slip through their fingers. On the other hand, Colson made a career of taking transfers and turning them into champions!

Front Row Left to right: Gene Deariso (Mgr.), Bill Moore, Ben Bates, Dan Petrovich, Bob Lamphier, Ron Fortner, Ernie Wood (Mgr.) Second Row : Jim Melvin (Assistant Coach), Mike Terry, Bryan Phillips, Gwendell McSwain, Paul Vick Russell Popham, Gary Colson (Head Coach)

When the Rebels took the court in the late fall of '66, their lineup looked like this: Ron Fortner, 6-2 junior, at point guard; Bob Lamphier, 6-3 junior, at shooting guard; Mike Terry, 6-5 junior, at small forward; Bryan Phillips, 6-6 junior, at center; Gwendell McSwain, 6-6 senior, at power forward; and Ben Bates, 6-2 senior, 6th man deluxe.

Floor Leadership was in capable hands once again, as the players selected Gwendell McSwain and Paul Vick captains. Vick was a senior, who was red-shirted last season, whom Colson counted on for leadership and depth. Everyone loved and respected the affable Vick, who was the walking definition of an unselfish team player if there was ever one in a Rebel uniform. As for McSwain, there's not enough time and space to write down how hard "Mac" played. While he was gifted athletically and size wise, it was his heart and head that made him a force to be reckoned with in the post (and elsewhere on the court). He was selfless to a fault, willing to set picks that enabled others to get wide open looks and was literally a "force of nature" on the boards, throwing his body at every rebound like it was his for the sake of the Rebels! Lamphier shares that "Mac was as great a person as he was a player" and that was why he was selected as one of the co-captains.

The schedule set up nicely for this edition of the Rebels, as they prepared to launch Colson's ninth campaign as the Rebel Head Coach. This group would be shooting for the Rebels' second Back-To-Back GIAC Championship and to kick the door down to claim the elusive District 25 Tournament Championship, and the ticket to Kansas City, home of the NAIA National Championship. Non-conference rivals

McSwain and Vick

FSU (one), JU (two), Oglethorpe (two), Tampa (two), and Georgia Southern (two) were on the docket. Those are nine tough games regardless of who you are, because they will be all out wars—no quarter given nor asked for!

The GIAC added Armstrong State, so there were 12 conference games, with Shorter (under Bill Foster) the chief challenger among the other six teams. Berry and West Georgia were overhauling their respective staffs to become competitive with the Rebels, as they were not content to get steamrolled every time they played the Rebels.

Take your memories back to 1966-67. The stage is set, the band is playing, and the crowd is getting louder upstairs; time to tip things off and get to the season highlights!

- Armstrong State College (Savannah) made its first trip to Titletown and ran right into a rampaging Rebel squad that easily won
  99-63.

- Next up in Tallahassee was the annual showdown with FSU. This game had become the 'Noles traditional opener. This year, they were led by new Head Coach Hugh Durham, who immediately began upgrading the Seminole roster. The game proved to be everything the media thought it would be, a war! The game began slowly. The Seminoles took control late in the first half and left the floor leading the Rebels, 35-25. As the second half opened, the Seminoles outscored the Rebels 9-4 in the first six minutes. As the Rebels had done historically under Colson, this group found that second gear and hit it hard. A Bates bucket with 7:51 left pulled the Rebels within two points, 54-52. With just ticks over five minutes left, McSwain put a layup in over the Dick Danford to knot the game at 54. A few possessions later, after the teams exchanged buckets, McSwain knocked down a 10-foot baseline jumper to give the Rebels their first lead of the game, 58-56, with 2:30 left. With a little less than one minute left, the 'Noles scored and a foul was called (a familiar refrain in this series), the Rebels were 1 down with the ball. A turnover and several FTs later, the Seminoles won another game where the Rebels walked away wondering what might have been. Mc-Swain had 18 and Terry 13 to lead the Rebels. With that said, this Rebels squad had established an identity—tough, aggressive, and relentless defensively. This group was "never going to give in." FSU was a solid team that struggled to score 60 points. On the other hand, the Rebels would need to improve their offensive execution and production, although all the pieces were there for that to happen shortly.
- The remainder of the fall schedule found the Rebels making progress on the offensive end, while continuing to be stingy on the defensive end. Although they overlooked and lost at home to a sound Tennessee College team, they rolled to an 8-2 record as the clash with Georgia Southern in Valdosta arrived. The Rebels blistered the Eagles by 24 points, 75-51, with McSwain and Phillips controlling the paint and the game. The Rebels' record

stood at 9-2 facing the next step toward a GIAC Championship with games against Shorter and Piedmont in Valdosta.

Bates (10), McSwain (15) Petrovich (42)

The schedule would have key non-conference games interspersed throughout the remainder of the GIAC schedule. Shorter proved as tough as expected, splitting the season series with the Rebels, losing 57-48 in Valdosta, and winning by two in Rome, 56-54. Foster had seen enough of the Rebels' running game and chose to slow the game down, limiting possessions. Berry had made commitments to improve and those changes began to show dividends this season, although they lost both games to the Rebels. The Rebels dispatched the other GIAC members in short order, running their GIAC record to 11-1 and the Rebels' second Back-To-Back GIAC Championship. The two losses were by a total of 4 points—keep that in mind as you read further.

• There were seven key non-conference games remaining after January: Oglethorpe (two), JU (two), Tampa (two), and Georgia Southern (one). The Rebels would split with Oglethorpe, winning 74-69 in Valdosta, and losing 57-56 in Atlanta. Tampa was beaten 82-74 in Valdosta, but won by four in Tampa, 67-63. Again, the two losses were by a total of 5 points. The Rebels went to Statesboro, where they had never beaten the Eagles. J.B. Scearce had announced he would step down as the head coach of the Eagles at the conclusion of the season. The legendary coach was loved by the fans and his players, so they would be playing with a little extra energy for their coach, and another chance to go to KC. The Rebels ruined the party, finding a way to squeeze a 69-66 win in the Eagles' lair and completing the season sweep over the hated District 25 rival and impediment to getting to KC! At this point, the record against the tough non-conference teams was 4-3. The three losses were at FSU by 3, at Oglethorpe by 1, and at Tampa by 4. JU rolled onto the calendar and schedule with a reloading effort taking place under Joe Williams and assistant coach Tom Wasden. They had taken over two years earlier, with the JU administration setting their sights on joining the NCAA, asking Williams and Wasden to take them in that direction. They had begun recruiting nationwide, with an emphasis in New York, Indiana, and Florida. They would have the Dolphins in the NCAA Championship game in the spring of '70. They showed up in Valdosta with players who would play in that championship game, Dan Hawkins (6-5 forward), Rex Morgan (6-5 guard), Ken Selke (6-7 forward), and Rod McIntyre (6-9 center). The game was nip and tuck all the way, although JU held a 5-7 point lead throughout the game. The Rebels were down 7 with just a breath over four minutes left in the game. The Rebels, as they had done against FSU earlier, proved to be resilient and relentless again, closing the gap to 2 points with possession of the ball with less than 15 seconds on the clock. The shot at the buzzer rimmed out and with it a chance to push the game into overtime. Lamphier led the Rebels with 19, Phillips had 15, Fortner 13, Terry 10, Bates 8, McSwain 5, and Petrovich 1. Bates and Phillips had 13 boards each, as the Rebels easily won the rebound battle 50-31. The game hinged on shooting efficiency. JU hit 53% from the floor and the Rebels slipped to 46%. The Rebels made their annual trip to Swisher Gym in Jacksonville and got waxed 99-74, the worst defeat of the season. For the regular season, the Rebels finished 4-5 against these nine opponents with the District 25 Tournament coming up on the horizon.

- The Rebels' overall record stood at 24-7 and 11-1 in the GIAC. Outside of the JU blowout victory, the other six losses were by a total of 16 points.
- The Rebels would play GIAC rival, Shorter, in the District 25

Tournament Championship Series (two out of three) with the first game in Rome. Lamphier hit the game winner. Those earlier difficult losses paid dividends as the Rebels proved resilient and relentless again, in Rome! "Never a bride, but a bridesmaid yet again!" Bill Foster's Hawks came to Valdosta with a huge target on their backs as the Rebel Nation unleashed a fury of sound like a Category 5 hurricane that would rival any arena today. The Rebels rolled in a blowout and had their ticket to KC punched for the first time ever!

(left to right) Bryan "Bigun" Phillips knocks down a 12' jumper. Mike Terry snatches another rebound. Gwendell McSwain soars for an easy block vs. Ga. Southern, as he controls the middle

• It was onto the airport and connection in Atlanta, then a direct flight into KC. For many in the Rebel travel party, it was their first flight. Definitely a dream come true for just about any player who has ever laced up a pair of converse sneakers—playing for a National Championship in a hallowed arena, Municipal Auditorium in downtown Kansas City. The Rebels were seeded #14 by the Dunkel Rating System, which meant they would play an unseeded team in the opening round. This year, it was Quincy from Illinois. The Rebels had entered the rare air—the round of 32. For those readers unfamiliar with how difficult it is to get to this point on Mt. Championship, consider there were over 300 teams at home who began this journey in October. The level of difficulty rises with every win in the postseason.

- The Rebels, who had split with Shorter during the season, had to turn around and beat them twice to get to Kansas City, which means they won three out four games this season against Shorter. No easy task to sweep teams at this level, much less beat them three times. Your reward is to play a team that on paper is better than Shorter in KC, although unranked. The next law of the postseason is beware of the unranked or lower-ranked teams in the early rounds. Lastly, for a handful of teams, this was not the first trip to KC, so their talent and experience in this five-day circus atmosphere is critical. Howard Payne (TX), Oklahoma Baptist, Eastern New Mexico, and St. Benedict's (Kan.) are examples of teams present in the 1967 National Tournament. In addition, Albany St. made the trip to KC through another District Tournament—two teams within 90 miles of one another in South Georgia make the final 32. On top of that, if both win their first two games, they square off in the Elite Eight (third round). Albany St. got beat in the first round.

- The Rebels beat Quincy convincingly, 78-64, to roll on into the Sweet 16 on their first trip to KC. That was the good news. The bad news is that the opponent in this round was third-seeded Oklahoma Baptist, which presented a formidable challenge. They had made it to the Final Four the previous two seasons and were led by their All American, Al Tucker. Tucker ended up the Tournament MVP this year (as well as last year), scoring 164 points in five games. The Rebels' season ended at the hands of this talented Oklahoma Baptist squad, 70-62. Oklahoma Baptist would make it to the finals for the third year in a row before falling to St. Benedict's, 71-62, who won their second National Championship. This time of year, in postseason play, only one team goes home smiling. To put the difficulties the Rebels (or any team) face at this level into context, consider that for St. Benedict, it was their second title in as many tries, behind Daryl Jones, their center who grabbed 62 rebounds in the five contests and effectively shut down other teams in the paint.

GIAC Champions	District 25 Champions	NAIA Sweet 16
• 1960-61	• 1966-67	• 1966-67
• 1961-62		
• 1962-63		
• 1963-64		
• 1965-66		
• 1966-67		

Season Highlights and Records:

- Overall record: 27-8, GIAC: 11-1. The Rebs' second Back-To-Back GIAC Championship and sixth in seven years.
- First NAIA District 25 Championship and first win at Kansas City, and first trip to the Sweet 16.
- Most points scored in a season in school history, 2,591. Was broken in 2018-19.
- Most FTs made in a season in school history, 599, still stands today.
- Most games won in a season, 27, was broken in 2009-10.

- Most rebounds in a season in school history, 407 by Bryan Phillips, still stands today!
- Best FT% in school history by Bob Lamphier, 86.2%, until it was broken in 2010-11.
- Leading scorers: Bryan Phillips (14.1), Mike Terry and Bob Lamphier (12.5 each).

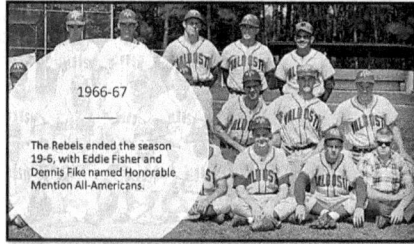

1966-67

The Rebels ended the season 19-6, with Eddie Fisher and Dennis Fike named Honorable Mention All-Americans.

A number of Rebels would move onto the baseball team: Bates, Fike, Fortner, and Lamphier, in the hopes of Back-to-Back Championships in baseball. The Rebels would end up in second place to West Georgia this year. McSwain and Bates would graduate. Otherwise, the Rebel starting lineup returned for their senior year: Fortner, Lamphier, Terry, and Phillips. They would be supplemented by the rising sophomores, especially John Trimnell and Robert McKinney. Colson and Melvin had a strategic plan whereby they would reload with a solid freshman class on a yearly basis, supplemented by transfers here and there. They had brought in a talented and deep freshman class in the fall of '66, so this spring and summer they could be more selective, as they were in position for a second Three-Peat and another District 25 Championship opportunity.

As Gary Colson's 10th season as head coach loomed on the horizon, the effervescent optimist had a number of reasons to be giddy about this group before preseason practice opened.

1967-68 A 2nd Three-peat. Back-to-Back District 25 Titles, and Aspirations to Make it Past the Sweet 16

Front Row. left to right: Glen Phelps (Mgr.), Mike Terry, Don Ward, Dale Croft, Robert McKinney, Bryan Phillips Second row: Jim Melvin (Assistant Coach), Grayson Hurley (Mgr.), Tommy Morrell, Paul O'Brien, John Trimnell, Jack Hart, Ron Fortner, Marty Lehman, Bob Lamphier, Gwendell McSwain (GA), Gary Colson(Head Coach)

First, his trusted and loyal assistant, Jim Melvin, was on board for the long haul, meaning he had continuity he never had from a Bench Leadership perspective. Colson and Melvin were both positive, optimistic and, in general, exceptionally effective with interpersonal relationship development and maintenance. Consequently, they were excellent recruiters! Both believed talent plus the Rebel Spirit were keys to winning consistently. Having talented players up and down the bench who were committed to the Rebel Spirit provided an edge most teams would not match. Between the two of them, they could develop the individual game for each player, as well as excel at that mysterious process called team building, and converting strategies into effectively executed plays during games. Colson focused his thoughts and energy on the offensive end and Melvin the defensive end. While the Rebels continued to operate out of the Wheel offensive system, Colson added wrinkles that would consistently frustrate opponents. Pinholster told Colson at breakfast (in front of Ritch) that "he (Pinholster) had invented the Wheel, but Colson perfected it!" Melvin had put in a couple of presses last season that were effective, a full-court press and a three-fourths-court press, that proved to be nightmares for opponents.

Second, he had the "4 horseman of the hardwood" back for their last rodeo: Fortner, Lamphier, Terry, and Phillips (the leading scorers and rebounders from the previous season). In essence, the core of last year's team returned. The two great losses were McSwain in the middle and Bates, one of the greatest 6th men in the history of Valdosta State. The coaching staff would have to find replacements from within the group of sophomores, since the staff determined they would go light on re-cruiting this year, signing one player, Marty Lehmann, a 6-4 wing from Gary, Indiana. Lehmann was athletic and could jump out of the gym, but needed to fine tune his game, so the jury was out on whether he would contribute this year.

It was apparent early on that 6-10 Robert McKinney, the tallest player in Valdosta State history, was the odds-on favorite to fill the slot left vacant by McSwain. McSwain says that "McKinney had an uncanny knack of being able to alter or block shots. He was the first player I had to account for when I was in the post, including Bill Pickens (6-10 All-American) from Georgia Southern."

Coach Colson's six, maybe seven-man rotation meant the 6th man had to be able to defend all five spots on the floor, rebound among the trees, handle the ball effectively, and shoot an efficient percentage so defenses had to account for them; all that to say John Trimnell would be the 6th man this season. And he more than lived up to expectations!

He was a rugged and tenacious defender/rebounder, as well as hav-ing an off-the-chart basketball IQ. Mike Perry described Trimnell "as the first guy you picked when you were playing pickup ball in the sum-mer and fall; otherwise, he was going to beat you. It didn't matter who got the first pick; Trimnell's name was called first because all he did was win baby!" Simply put, John Trimnell was a champion!

That left two sophomores, Dale Croft and Paul O'Brien, next in line. Croft was exceptionally talented, although he lacked the consistent ef-fort Colson wanted to see. When he wanted to elevate his game, he was as good as the Rebels had had on the wing. O'Brien was an athletic and ambidextrous point guard, who could literally handle the ball and shoot with either hand. He ran track in high school as well as basketball, so his first step and leaping ability were powerful weapons. Since Fortner was a senior point guard, unless foul trouble or injuries got in the way, Fortner would see at least 90% of the minutes at that slot.

It is important to understand Colson's player development strategy once he began to develop roster depth and balance, recruiting a year or two ahead of his needs. For example, Ritch did not start immediately his freshman year and neither did Mike Perry, both Valdosta State Hall of Famers. Perry said, "I did very little to contribute my first year, but I did learn incredible lessons from what I saw during games and from playing against the upperclassmen at practice." Fortner and Lamphier showed up as freshmen, learning from their experiences at practice and watching the upperclassmen compete. Lamphier reflects on that first year: "I learned so much watching Ray, Letson, and Bobby play hard and smart, executing efficiently over and over on both ends of the floor. That time to learn and reflect was invaluable and made me a better player."

Marty Lehmann, who arrived in the fall of '67, provides more details of the rookie experience under Colson:

"The '67-'68 team was a veteran team, with four seniors and two sophomores. They had the whole package: size, speed, smarts, and strength, as well as the Rebel Spirit. You had to be smart to play for Gary Colson, because the offense he ran, the Wheel, was detailed and somewhat complicated

Coach Melvin and Coach Colson

at first, but was so effective it facilitated the Rebels' dominance within the GIAC. The manner in which Colson and Melvin taught us to run the offense made us more disciplined, resilient—tougher and smarter than our opponents. Learning it as a freshman was hard. Colson's and Melvin's ability to teach it was terrific. They were patient, offering insights and reasons why cuts had to be made here, not there. Why picks had to be set here, not there. Their instruction included enhancing your ability to cut so you would get open, how to set a pick to spring the cutter, and there were literally any number of alternative routes and screens that could be taken. They laid out the drills by position. Their drills were repetitive in nature and with enough live action so we would have examples to learn from. If you learned it to the point it was second nature, then a whole new world of basketball opened up.

A big key to learning it came from the upperclassmen, who willingly helped educate you—a vital part of the Rebel culture developed and nurtured by Coach Colson and Coach Melvin. I was lucky to have guys like Phillips, Trimnell, Fortner, etc., who would bend over backwards to help me! I have to add that those same seniors appeared to take some particular glee in using the Wheel as an instrument of torture on unsuspecting rookies, like me. There were some particularly vicious screens set and the beatings would continue until you developed that 6th sense and acquired knowledge of the patterns within the offense. In between getting your feet wet and crossing the line of experience, it felt like I was falling out of a huge redwood tree, hitting every branch on the way down. As time went along, I learned when and how to deal with those blind screens; more importantly, friendships formed between me and the upperclassmen, and I took my place as a Rebel."

Preseason practice found the rookies and others being matched against Colson's 6-7 man rotation. Lehmann, along with Tommy Morrell, Don Ward, Jack Hart, and Dale Croft, formed what was referred to as the "Rifle Squad." The starters and rotation looked like this:

- Co-Captain Bryan Phillips a 6-6, 250 pound center, was an All-Conference player who was as adept outside as he was inside. He was a mismatch for most centers and power forwards of that era. While having an exquisite shooting touch from 20 feet, he was particularly tough on the glass—more like a bull in a china closet.

- Co-Captain Mike Terry was a 6-5 forward and another All-Conference player. Colson called Terry "the best 15-18-foot shooter I have ever coached." He was a relentless defensive player and rebounder. Marty Lehmann says Terry "made more unusual shots than anyone he has ever seen. In a single game, he had a ball hit his shoulder and go in for a bucket. Same game, he knocked the ball away from the opponent into the basket."
- Bob Lamphier, a 6-3 guard/forward, (and All Conference) with an incredible touch from deep. His shots looked as if they were launched on the far end of a rainbow and followed the arc perfectly to the bottom of the net.

Bryan Phillips (45) and Mike Terry (30)

- Ron Fortner, a 6-2 point guard, All Conference, was the "glue that made this team great. He ran the show, if you were willing, you could learn what a point guard should do to lead the team and manage the game." (M. Lehmann)

- Robert McKinney was a 6-10 sophomore center, but was untested at the varsity level. He had an effective 19-foot shooting range, which made him a matchup problem when the Rebels ran the Wheel.
- John Trimnell was 6-2 with the linebacker's body and mentality. His basketball IQ was unparalleled, as was his tenacity and willingness to take on and overcome any challenging assignment. He was a utility player who could play any of the five positions effectively, although this year his energy off the bench would prove to be a key ingredient. He could handle the ball, rebound among the trees, defend the best player, and was willing to shoot the key shot when it mattered.

The schedule for this powerful squad of Rebels was loaded, as usual. The non-conference schedule included the usual rivals: Tampa (two), Georgia Southern (two), FSU (one), and Oglethorpe (two). In addition were tournament games against West Florida, Chattanooga, Pembrooke (NC), and Frederick (Virginia). Eleven games against District Tournament caliber teams. The Rebels had to be ready to go! Basketball in this region of the Southeast was in the national spotlight due to the developments at FSU and JU, two programs that would challenge for NCAA crowns over the next three years.

The GIAC remained the same, 12 games. The chief rivals were Shorter and Berry, with LaGrange and West Georgia becoming more competitive. The trip to Piedmont was always a tough out and while an undermanned Georgia Southwestern seemed a mismatch, their head coach was adept at maxing out his team's performance against the Rebels.

The Rebels were inconsistent early, unable to win some close contests. They were upset by West Florida at home, 76-75. The Rebels proved resilient and bounced back to beat Chattanooga soundly, 80-68. Mike Terry led the Rebels in scoring in these two games, tallying 16 and 28 points in the respective games. The Rebels jumped all over Armstrong State, 85-64, in their 1st conference game of the year. That victory was followed up by a demolition of Georgia State, 92-64. The overall record stood at 3-1 as they hit the road for a tournament in NC, where they proceeded to lose two in a row, 79-61 and 80-78. Their record slipped to 3-3, but more importantly, they had lost two of the three games by a meager 3 points. Returning home for their tournament, the Rebels won three in a row before they drove to Tampa to face Dana Kirk's Tampa Spartans. Lehmann describes what playing at Tampa was like in those days, "When you played at their place, you were down by 15 before you put on the uniform." The Rebels delivered a valiant and hard fought effort that found them down one, 62-61, with seconds left on the clock and the ball out under Tampa's basket. Colson drew up a play where Bryan Phillips would appear to set a back pick for Fortner, who would come to receive the ball in the backcourt. Fortner actually set a pick that sprung the big "tight end looking" Phillips for a full-court pass from Trimnell. The play worked like a charm. Phillips was wide open, and Trimnell's throw appeared on the money, until it hit the lowest ceiling lights in modern basketball history. Fate was unkind to these Rebels again, losing by one point when they knew in their hearts, they should have won that game! Their record stood at 6-4, with three of the losses by 4 total points.

- As the Rebels approached the mid-point of the season, they buried Piedmont, 112-68, blew past Berry, 77-63, and West Georgia, 91-64. Their GIAC record stood at 4-0, then losing to Georgia Southern and Oglethorpe, on the road. They would return to Valdosta to beat Georgia State and blast Piedmont (GIAC record now 5-0), before facing the sternest test of the season, nationally ranked FSU.
- Hugh Durham was in the midst of building a monster program in Tallahassee. Durham's second season pivoted around a talented group of sophomores, including 6-8 Dave Cowens (future Celtic great and NBA HOF) among others. Durham had played for FSU under Bud Kennedy, then served as a grad assistant and assistant before moving into the Head Coach's seat. His first two recruit-

ing classes were talented to say the least. Tully Gymnaisum was rocking when the Rebels showed up and Durham made sure the 'Noles were aware of the last time the two squads tangled, with the 'Noles eking out a narrow victory in the last few seconds.

Fortner (13) Terry (30)

Cowens managed a double-double, with 23 points to go along with 17 rebounds (it was always a mystery when you watched tape of the FSU games, you could never find as many rebounds for him as the Official Scorer did, but I digress). The 'Noles won 81-71, on their way to the NCAA Tournament and a couple of monumental clashes with JU. Bryan Phillips had a great game, 26 points and 8 rebounds in a valiant effort against an imposing frontline. Bigun' described the game and his strategy "as tough, physical, and aggressive. I did everything I could to make it tough on Cowens. Charlie Bloodworth was the lead official and let us play. It was the kind of game I believe Cowens and I preferred—physical and aggressive." Cowens' numbers were lower than usual, which reflected the work Bigun' did in the paint that night!

Mike Terry played a great game, pouring in 19 points and hauling in 9 rebounds. Ron Fortner was under duress the entire night, since Durham loved full-court pressure in a variety of forms, as he scored 10 points and snagged 6 rebounds. This was by far a better Seminole team than the Rebels had faced previously. Durham had them on track to challenge for an NCAA title shortly (1971). With that said, the Rebels played gallantly in the face of this overwhelming force!

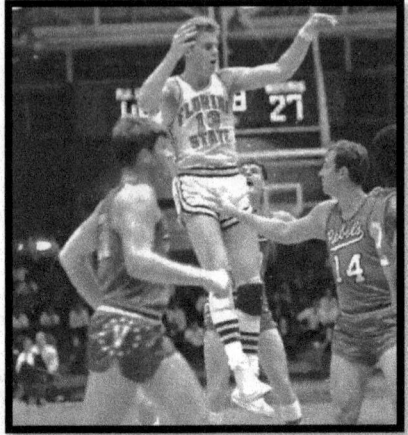

Dave Cowens of FSU leaps over Trimnell and Dale Croft

The Rebels would leave the FSU game in the rearview mirror, being the resilient bunch they were when they traveled to Carrollton and LaGrange. Both games were hard fought, as the Rebels won both, moving their GIAC record to 6-0 and setting up a rematch with the Georgia Southern Eagles in Valdosta. Bob Lamphier put up 22 points to lead the Rebels to a convincing 68-48 win over a District rival.

Bryan Phillips receiving the District trophy from President Martin

∘ The next segment of the season saw the Rebels beat LaGrange and Georgia Southwestern in Valdosta. LaGrange made life miserable for the Rebels, who had to mount a second half comeback led by Terry's 22 points and Phillips 20 points. Robert McKinney was a menace to LaGrange, grabbing a game-high 22 rebounds, blocking 10 shots, and scoring 11 points—his first triple/double of his career. The Rebels headed to Rome to face Berry and Shorter with an 8-0 conference slate. The Rebels had managed to handle the upstart Vikings of Berry in Valdosta but ran into a buzz saw in Rome, losing 62-52. They righted the ship and beat Shorter to regain any lost momentum and solidify their stranglehold on the conference race with two games left against Armstrong State and Georgia Southwestern, whom they handled easily, finishing the GIAC slate with an 11-1 record and a third-straight conference championship and 7th in eight years. That left two non-conference games at home against rivals Oglethorpe and Tampa. Oglethorpe escaped with a one point win, 61-60, to dampen the momentum the Rebels had built over the last four weeks (since FSU). The Rebels again proved resilient, holding off Tampa in a nail-biter, 57-56. It was their first win of the year by that tight a margin. They had lost four games by 5 points, but as great teams do, they learn from those experiences and at the end of the season, they flipped the script .

◦ The postseason had become a tradition since Colson's third year, and this season would prove to be another great run for the Rebels! First off, the Rebels faced Augusta College in the District 25 Tournament, where the victor had to win two out of three to claim the ticket to KC. The first game was played in Augusta. Augusta had come into its own over the last 2-3 years in basketball; they were your typical District Championship opponent—athletic, physical, and skilled. The Rebels headed to the Jaguars' den in Augusta and came away with a hard fought 60-55 win in an extremely hostile environment. The Rebels never wavered, just simply out-executed the Jags, and knocked them onto the canvas. The second game was played in front of a raucous Rebel Nation, who were eagerly anticipating the tip-off every time "Going to Kansas City" was played over the sound system. The game was never in doubt as the Rebels cruised to an 84-56 demolition of a strong Augusta squad. Chalk that victory up to fans like Red Cross and Rebel Nation, who had the noise level somewhere around a jet engine revving for takeoff! The seniors delivered in the clutch: Fortner had 21, Phillips 19, Terry 14, and Lamphier 11. They won the District 25 Championship two years in a row!

The Rebels headed to the airport to catch the connection flight to Atlanta and onto Kansas City with the 14th seed in their pocket once again. Their first-round opponent was the unseeded (actually, they were probably the 30th seed out of 32) Westmar College Eagles (Iowa). The Rebels managed a clean victory, 62-57, with Fortner leading the scoring brigade with 18, followed by McKinney with 16. The 14 seed always faces off with the third seed if they advance. In this case, the Rebels took on the Central State Marauders (Ohio), a group that had one Fab Four appearance and National Championship under their belt. The Marauders were a gritty, grind it out, physical outfit. They beat the Rebels at their own game—defense and disciplined offense—to win 60-53. The Rebels were led by Phillips, Fortner, and Terry with 10 points each. The Marauders would go on to win their second National Championship, defeating Fairmont State, 51-48. The 53 points the Rebels scored against the Marauders were the most scored against them in the last four rounds of this tournament.

Colson's 10th season at the helm was nothing less than outstanding!

- Overall, the Rebels finished 23-10 and 11-1 in the GIAC. Colson's record over the decade was an outstanding 176-73 (71%) overall and 93-23 in the GIAC (80%).
- The Rebels' first objective every year was to win the GIAC, which they did for the third year in a row (Colson's second Three-Peat); having won the conference 7 out of 8 years since 1960.
- The second objective every season was to win the District 25

Championship. The Rebels won the District 25 Championship Back-To-Back in 1967 and 1968, becoming only the second school to turn that trick in the decade of the 60s, the other being Georgia Southern (who reached the finals before losing). The competition for the District 25 Championship was stout during that decade because it included schools from Florida and Georgia (Stetson, JU, and Georgia Southern). Valdosta State, Stetson, and Georgia Southern are the only schools to move past the first round in KC.

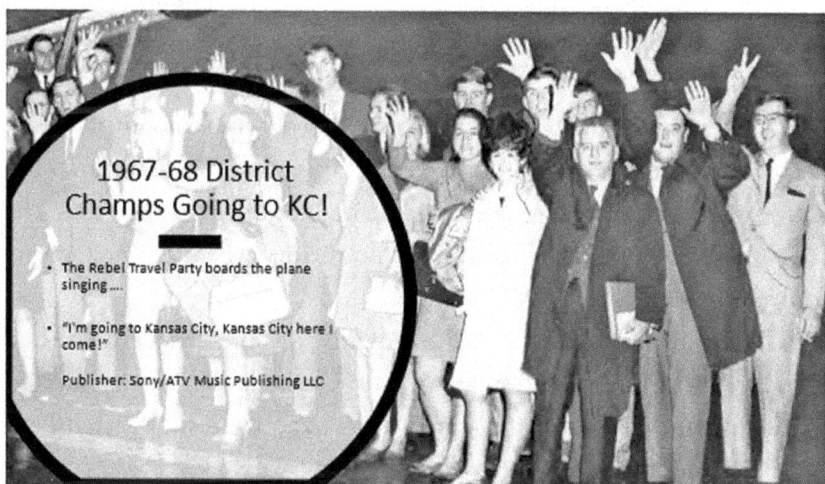

1967-68 District Champs Going to KC!

- The Rebel Travel Party boards the plane singing....

- "I'm going to Kansas City, Kansas City here I come!"

Publisher: Sony/ATV Music Publishing LLC

- Postseason honors were received by Bryan Phillips, All Conference – All District and 3rd Team NAIA All American. Mike Terry, Bob Lamphier, and Ron Fortner were All Conference as well.

- The leading scorers for the Rebels were Terry at 17.3 ppg and Phillips with 14.5 ppg.

- Terry completed an illustrious four-year career for the Rebels playing and starting in 116 games (both school records), scoring 1,599 points (13.8 ppg) for 5th place on the school's 1,000 point club, and being inducted into the Valdosta State Hall of Fame.

- Lamphier's outstanding four-year career ended with him owning the highest FT percentage in school history, 86.2%.

- The Senior Class of Fortner, Lamphier, Terry, and Phillips won three GIAC titles, two District 25 Championships, and won both first-round games in KC. Their overall four-year record was 90-27, and in the GIAC their record was 40-4; one of the most accomplished Senior Classes in school history.

As the basketball season closed down, Danny Petrovich and Ron Fortner headed to the baseball diamond to join their teammates in preparation for the upcoming baseball season, which found the Rebels finishing 15-9 under new Head Coach Tommy Thomas. Petrovich earned Honorable Mention All American honors for his efforts on the diamond.

Finally, a major off-season change occurred, which potentially impacted both the GIAC and District 25 races in the near future. The change was a surprise on one hand, but not totally unexpected on the other. Colson accepted the Head Coach position at Pepperdine University, soon to be located in Malibu, CA.

Colson's college friend, Dr. Bill Banowsky, was the President and had an audacious vision for the small, private Christian University located at that time in Inglewood, CA. Banowsky's vision was simply that Pepperdine would be the preeminent small, conservative institution on the west coast of the US. One of his key strategies in this bold change management endeavor was to rebuild the athletic program. That's where Gary Colson came in. Dr. Banowsky knew Colson was a builder and developer of championship cultures. Dr. Banowsky and the Chancellor, M. Norvel Young, secured a huge piece of land in a gift from the Rindge Family in Malibu where they would build the new campus. Once the deal for the land in Malibu was closed, they offered Colson the job. It was an opportunity he could not turn down—another building project in a top tier mid-major conference, the West Coast Athletic Conference. The WCAC a decade earlier had seen K.C. Jones and Bill Russell win not only the conference, but national championships while at the University of San Francisco.

Coach Colson's departure was not totally unexpected, considering the success he had developing the Rebel program from a club level to a national presence. In the coaching industry, at any level, when you accomplish what Coach Colson accomplished, there will be interest from other programs. It was a step forward in Colson's coaching career, the big stage, Los Angeles, and a chance to make history again at a small college.

The Gary Colson Decade: A Catalyst to Building a Championship Culture

Gary Colson accomplished far more than even he envisioned when he signed on to coach the Rebels. The following list is not meant to cover 100% of his accomplishments, but to provide a sense of the breadth and scope of the outcomes under Colson's leadership:

- His overall record was 176-73 and within the GIAC 93-23.
- His teams won the GIAC seven out of his last eight years, accomplishing a Four-Peat from 1961-1964 and a Three-Peat from 1966-68. The Rebels dominated the GIAC during Colson's tenure, winning 80% of their games and going undefeated twice (in back-to-back seasons, '61 and '62).
- Colson's last two teams, '67 and '68, won the District 25 Championship. These two teams also won first-round games in Kansas City moving onto the Sweet 16, where they lost to the eventual National Champion and Finalist.
- The graduation rate under Coach Colson's watch was close to 100%, indicative of character of players recruited to play for the Rebels. If someone left before they finished their academic degree, they could return, and Colson would demonstrate his loyalty by making sure they could finish what they started.
- Valdosta State had received an incredible amount of press throughout the Southeast, due to Rebel basketball success (from the Atlanta Journal Constitution, Florida Times-Union, Valdosta Daily Times, etc.). Dr. Martin noted such in his yearly re-

port to the Georgia Board of Regents in 1968, explaining that "the Intercollegiate athletic program is one of the college's tools for good public relations. We have been greatly pleased with the fine response received from those who have seen our teams in action. These young gentlemen have brought widespread recognition to the college through their behavior and competitive abilities." Dr. Martin then described the success of the most recent Rebel basketball team. As one reads the report, it is clear the number of applications increased nearly 40% year-over-year and enrollment was up 25% YOY. While there are a number of reasons for the increases in enrollment, historical research notes that success by universities and colleges in the athletic realm, along the ensuing media notoriety, positively impacts application flow and enrollment. The consistent success the Rebels had over the duration of Colson's decade was a significant factor to the elevation of the overall profile of Valdosta State, which fed enrollment that swelled from 500-600 in the early 1960s to over 2,500 by the end of the decade.

- In the words of Mike Perry, Colson "took what was basically a club team and turned it into a juggernaut within the GIAC and eventually, District 25." When Colson started operations in the spring of '58, the Rebels could not beat Oglethorpe or Georgia Southern. By 1968, the Rebels had pulled even and maybe held a slight edge on both programs, as evidenced by Back-to-Back District Championships.

- Colson came aboard as the Head Basketball and Tennis Coach, as well as taught a couple of PE classes every quarter. For the better part of eight years, he worked these 2-3 jobs and was able to piece together a staff of part-time assistant and graduate assistant, plus a manager. He did this without the benefit of a secretary or administrative assistant. By the time he left for Pepperdine, he had earned a full-time assistant coach position. What he was able to do with limited funding and staff cannot be understated or glossed over. Most head coaches in today's world focus solely on the sport they are coaching.

In 10 years, Colson built a championship culture and program that was on the way to becoming a dynasty within their conference and region from scratch. Valdosta State became a destination for players and staff who wanted to compete for championships at the highest level!

Colson left the whispering pines of South Georgia and the Rebel Basketball program better than he found it 10 years before. He gave it all he had while he was in Valdosta and it made all the difference. In the end, that is what matters!

GIAC Champions	District 25 Champions	NAIA Sweet 16
• 1960-61	• 1966-67	• 1966-67
• 1961-62	• 1967-68	• 1967-68
• 1962-63		
• 1963-64		
• 1965-66		
• 1966-67		
• 1967-68		

8

❧

The Melvin Years: Successfully Navigating the Winds of Change

Introduction

Dr. Walter Martin, who replaced Dr. Thaxton as the President at VSC two years prior, did not waste much time interviewing and naming Jim Melvin the third Head Coach of the Rebels within days. Melvin had the requisite and relevant experience to not only provide continuity and consistency within the basketball program, but the skill set to address the challenges (external and internal) brought on by the coaching change.

The customary internal cultural challenges associated within any organizational changes at the top were reduced with Melvin's appointment. Jim Melvin wanted to play and coach at Valdosta State. He explained that he "dreamed as a young child of playing at Valdosta State. Then my aspirations evolved to emulating Gary Colson, and coach at Valdosta State." William Ward once said, "if you can imagine it, you can achieve it. If you can dream it, you can become it;" which certainly applied to Melvin, who played for Colson for two years, serving as a coach on the floor at point guard and leading the Rebels to an undefeated season within the GIAC and their first GIAC title. Coach Melvin returned as an Assistant Coach in the spring of 1966, serving Colson and the Rebels the last two seasons. Melvin understood, cherished, and embraced the Rebel Championship culture, as well as the expectations that went along with it. Consequently, there would be a smooth transition between Colson and Melvin from a continuity of culture perspective.

Jim Melvin's Background, Leadership Skill Set and Management Style

Whereas Gary Colson arrived and served as a catalyst that transformed a club team into a championship dynasty, Melvin's role as a leader and the challenges he would face were somewhat different. While the new head coach needed to retain the core elements of the championship culture, his challenges were to navigate the internal challenges created by the coaching change, as well as addressing external challenges associated with the pending integration of the athletic program, while continuing to win championships (GIAC and District 25). Melvin's personality, leadership skills, and style would prove Dr. Martin's choice was spot on! In short order, Coach Melvin took control of the situation by conveying a clear vision of the team's goals, demonstrated a marked passion in addressing any challenges at hand, and an uncanny ability to make the staff and team feel recharged and energized. These are the behaviors a Transformational Leader demonstrates in facing the winds of change.

Jim Melvin humbly claims he is from "8½ miles southwest of Plains, off a dirt road, off another dirt road, etc." Growing up on a farm, he had time to hone his basketball skills after working. He says, "he always wanted to be the best player ever at Plains HS," again demonstrating his aspirations were always elevated. He started as a freshman, unheard of at PHS at the time, and teamed up with their All State 6-10 center to become a regular participant in the Georgia State Playoffs all four years. He spent two successful years at Georgia Southwestern before the opportunity he had been praying and hoping for arrived in the mail—the offer to play for the beloved Rebels. Little did he realize he was just beginning to touch the hem of his aspirations!

Melvin spent two years playing under Colson, which he describes as "magical!" The Rebels went undefeated and were champions of the GIAC in Melvin's last year! Melvin describes Coach Colson as one of his role models, "Gary was charismatic, a great recruiter, smart, and enthusiastic! I wanted to be like him!" Another opportunity to learn from the best existed in Valdosta at the time, Wright Bazemore, the legendary head football coach at VHS. Coach Melvin explained "I would go to Wildcat practices at every opportunity to learn how Bazemore was able to win championships over sustained periods of time. That is where I learned that winning is the natural by-product of properly executing the fundamentals." Melvin coached at Mitchell County HS before leaving to work on his Master's degree at the University of Georgia. While there, he served as Assistant Coach of the Freshman Team.

As he wound up his Master's in the spring of '66 and began planning to return to Valdosta State as Colson's assistant, fate's hand intervened in an unusual manner. Bryan Phillips, who was loaded with unlimited potential, was in the process of leaving the University of Georgia. Coach Melvin knew Bryan and called Colson. Both Philips and Coach Melvin joined the Rebels for the 1966-67 campaign. Chalk up another recruiting coup for Colson! It was also the second time Melvin had recommended a transfer to Colson, the first being Homer Chambliss. Melvin knew talent when he saw it, the necessary gift any successful college coach has to have.

Melvin's leadership philosophy is simple, but highly effective: "Put the players in a position where they can excel with their gifts, reinforce the behavior you want, and play solid, fundamental basketball." Coach Melvin later explained "that meant we needed to get Jimmy Dorsett and

Joe Brogdon all the 15-18-foot jump shots we can find, and man did they fill it up!" He sought to learn everyone's gifts, accentuate, and reinforce them, and let them know how that could help the team.

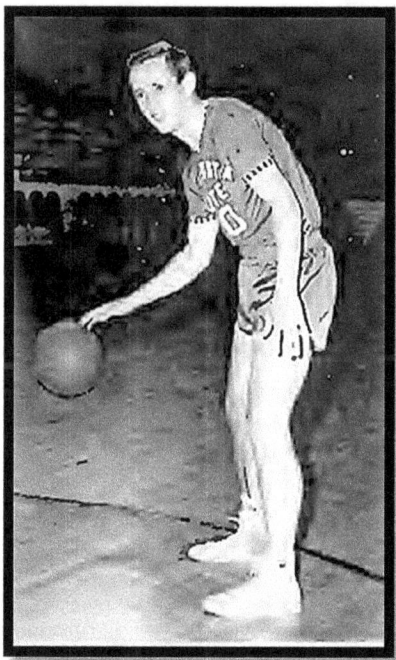

Jim Melvin as VSC player

He was a leader who was aspirational in every sense of the word, always setting elevated expectations of the team and individuals within the culture! He had an uncanny ability to think outside of the box regarding what his teams and players could accomplish. He could envision what could be rather than what is, then articulate that vision, encouraging everyone along the way, and letting nothing stand in the way. The 1968-69 team is a great example: Who would have thought that a team with just six players in the rotation (the tallest 6-6, the others were 6-2 and 6-4 Marty Lehmann coming off the bench) was destined to become GIAC (undefeated) and District 25 Champions? He infused confidence into the team, "that collectively they could play with anyone, regardless of their talent and size." In turn, that team reflected the coaching staff's trust and confidence, winning games against teams where they were mismatched in size night in and night out.

There are many examples of how his aspirational visions affected individuals (and then the team). Here are two people, one a player and the other a manager/trainer, who would go on to be selected co-captains in 1970-71 by their teammates.

Marty Lehmann had little experience when Melvin took over. In fact, Lehmann remembers the one-on-one meeting he had with Coach Melvin in the spring of '68 after Coach Melvin took over. "He told me he was not sure about me yet. Then challenged me to work on my game over the next five months." Melvin said, "after the discussion with Marty in the spring of '68, he and I played one on one after every workout, at times for a couple of hours. He was committed to getting his game to the next level." Melvin's unique ability and insight to stir the soul of his players was clear. By Christmas, Lehmann was a lightning rod of a 6th man. He played quicker and bigger than his 6-4, 185-pound frame appeared. Lehmann defended all positions, played the point on the full-court press, and banged with the "bigs" to get rebounds with every ounce of his being. When he came on to the floor, the energy and intensity level amped up dramatically on the floor and in the stands. He played beyond his experience, size, and skill set throughout his career!

Melvin was not a leader who would step over a stone. He was the leader who left no stone unturned in his efforts to enhance (+1) what Colson had started. Coach Colson had Syrup Deariso as a manager and "Mr. Fix It" for 2 years (and took him to Pepperdine). Melvin re-cruited Fred Gibbons from North Florida JC after seeing him energize his NFJC teammates during a game where the coach was evaluating a player. Coach Melvin had not come seeking a manager/trainer. Later, Coach Melvin explained to Gibbons "that his energy, enthusiasm, and never-say-die attitude was infectious and just what the Rebels need from the sidelines every day. Your attitude and example will make a difference to this team!" Gibbons describes the effect this conversation had on his life and career: "No one (not parents, physical therapist, other coaches) ever encouraged and empowered me like he did that day. For the first time, I saw how I could be more than the guy who washes uniforms and tapes ankles—that I could make a difference!" Lehmann shares his take on Gibbons' impact on him, as well as the team: "Our new manager/trainer was super fired up and competitive, as solid a teammate as I've ever had on or off the floor. He was an inspiration to me and others every day. He had contracted polio as a child, wore a brace on his left leg, and had to work hard to walk. He never once com-plained when we were training. He trained along with us, working as hard or harder than we did. If you loafed, he would call you out, from the day he arrived, he made us better!"

Melvin would face a stiff test in enhancing the championship tradition created during the Colson era. Cultures tend to change their tone and direction from one leader to the next, often eroding performance, production, and the results people are used to seeing. For example, UCLA is still searching for the next John Wooden, just as Alabama searched in the wilderness for 30+ years for the next Bear Bryant. Cultures and programs in the midst of searching through the wilderness often incur losses stacked on losses. Suffice it to say, replacing a leader at the top by another does not guarantee success.

Melvin did not need to be a catalyst for change. He needed to navigate the winds of change—the ensuing turbulent currents that created internal and external challenges as he took over the helm of the vaunted Rebel basketball program. He would be more than up to the task!

Melvin Sets Sail Toward Another Championship Season

Externally, there were various perspectives on the change in leadership of the Rebel basketball program. Internally, what made this change of leadership challenging, as well as intriguing, was that recent titles were won with teams that were upperclassmen laden, the core of which graduated that spring. While GIAC rivals were licking their chops, Rebel fans and boosters were curious what the effects would be, especially since all five starters graduated or left school. Yet, Melvin was as cool as the other side of a pillow, never blinking, just going about his business!

There were multiple objectives on the new head coach's agenda: complete the recruiting of a potential All-American, hire an assistant coach, and stabilize the returning set of players. Melvin was in the Atlanta area in late February (by this point, Coach Melvin was aware of the possibility Colson was leaving) as the high school playoffs opened, looking at a couple of talented prospects. He saw Dykes HS play and was struck with the teamwork, relentless defensive effort, and their overall discipline. Dykes was coached by James Dominey (in his first year), who had brought this program back from the bottom of their league to double-digit wins. Melvin, knowing what he was looking for in an assistant, met with Dominey after the game. He explained the situation in Valdosta—that he might be named the head coach, and would he (Coach Dominey) be interested in the assistant job? Dominey said yes, and Jim Melvin made the phone call shortly after being named head coach. His proactive leadership meant he had who he was looking for in an assistant.

Jim Melvin's humility is reflected in the choice of Coach Dominey, who was one of the bright, young minds in Georgia basketball at the time. Their personalities and styles complemented one another, which enhanced every aspect of the Rebel program. Melvin had found a young, gifted, relentless hard worker who was passionate about the game (especially the defensive end). Although they were both under 30 years old at the time, they were energetic, passionate, intelligent, and innovative, and they would become one of the formidable coaching tandems in the Southeast, if not the nation!

They would need every ounce of their coaching skills and leadership abilities since expectations were set higher than ever. GIAC championships were a regular event (seven out of the last eight years under Colson), but were only the first step toward a NAIA District 25 Championship (the Rebels had won the last two in a row) and the coveted trip to Kansas City to play for a National Championship. The young coaches would prove to be up to the challenge!

The second objective on Melvin's agenda was bringing a potential All-American into the Rebel fold. As the 1967-68 season wound down, Melvin and Colson had been intensely recruiting a sensational player from Albany, 6-6 Pete Smith. Smith had left the University of Cincinnati after the fall semester in '67. Colson and Melvin invited Smith to come to Valdosta to watch the '68 District Championship game versus Augusta, then work out. He was an extremely talented ball player, one who could score from anywhere on the floor, rebound, block shots, and handle the ball. He had a 36-inch vertical leap, playing around 6-10 when fully extended. In other words, if he fronted the low post, the wing had to throw it to the top of the glass to get it over him. Yet, Smith was quick enough to play the back end of the full-court press by himself. Any pass thrown from the end line to the other side of half court was going to get picked off and brought back in a hurry. In short, Smith was a generational talent.

James Melvin and Assistant Coach James Dominey

The leadership challenge Melvin faced with Smith was the integration of the basketball program. Although Dr. Thaxton facilitated the integration of the college in 1963, the athletic program had not yet made that step. How would the team, as well as the community, accept and thrive with this crucial step that would serve as a beacon of societal growth for the community, college, and the athletic program? Melvin proactively and positively navigated these tricky external social culture currents without tipping over the program's progress! How?

First, Coach Melvin for years demonstrated and developed trust and respect among the high school coaches of all races within southwest Georgia. He was personable, genuine and developed solid relationships with coaches, especially in the Albany area. Having coached in this part of Georgia, he was well known and highly respected.

Second, he developed a solid relationship with Smith on the recruiting trail—Pete trusted and respected Coach Melvin.

Third, he received the support of the team leaders who would be returning. Check out Marty Lehmann's (who would be returning as a sophomore the next season) description of how the workout and ensuing events transpired on page 129. The workout was set up after the District 25 Championship game with Augusta in Valdosta. The recruitment of Pete Smith by Coach Melvin, as well as his room assignment with John Trimnell, facilitated an easy assimilation of Smith into the Rebel program and culture.

Fourth, Smith was not only an incredible athlete whose ceiling included the NBA, but more importantly, his warm personality and street smarts meant the assimilation with the team and community would be smoother. In recruiting Smith, Melvin had successfully landed what many analysts refer to as one of the top 10 players in the Southeast at the time, including high school and college. Pete Smith later earned team MVP, GIAC MVP, and Honorable-Mention All American honors. He was drafted by both the NBA and ABA.

Moreover, Melvin's leadership and interpersonal relationship-building skills had a profound effect on facilitating further integration at Valdosta State, as well as the Valdosta community in general. His close relationship with the Rome brothers (Stan and Roger) reflected the trust and respect he gave to everyone, regardless of race. They were in the gym and locker room frequently. Both were 5-star recruits, stars in football and basketball at Valdosta HS. Both still love and respect him, including him in their recent book describing their life!

By the time May rolled around, Coach Melvin's ability to acquire James Dominey as the Assistant Coach and recruit Pete Smith out from under Albany State answered the anxious questions surrounding the Rebel program.

Now, he and Coach Dominey could turn their focus on filling out the remainder of the roster and begin developing the players who

> *"The members of the Rifle squad were asked to stay after the game and scrim-mage with a recruit. Anytime we were asked to participate in a tryout, it meant our job was on the line next year and maybe for our career. Consequently, we played hard in those affairs because we were playing for our jobs. Team or no team, we took it personal. As we came back up the stairs and entered the gym, we saw a number of boosters on the far end of the floor, which was unusual for a tryout. On the far end of the floor was this 6-6 African-American guy shooting around. We were introduced to Pete and it did not take long for all of us to learn how talented he was. He could shoot from anywhere, handle the ball and jump over the backboard. He left every one of us speechless after the scrimmage, he was that great a player.... then he enrolls and becomes Trimnell's roommate during the Spring Quarter '68."* Marty Lehmann

would be returning for the coming season, although that list was lim-ited due to transfers and academic suspensions. Trimnell was the only returning player with significant playing time, as the 6th man. There was lots of work to do to complete the roster between May and September.

9

1968-69 - 8th GIAC Championship and three-peat in District 25 Championship

1968-69: The Rebel Express Roars Out of Nowhere to Win Their 8th GIAC Championship and a Three-Peat in the District 25 Championship

As the sultry heat and humidity of late August soared above the 100-degree heat index in the old gym during those summer evening workouts and pick-up games, one of the lingering questions was whether John Trimnell would make it back for Fall Registration without being drafted by the military. That single question raised the heat index in the coach's office a couple of degrees because JT was a critical player to the coming season's Rebels. As the calendar raced toward Fall Registration, it became clear the "Duck" (his nickname because he walked like a duck) would return to campus, and the coaches (and players) breathed a huge sigh of relief!

To set the stage for this season, first consider the schedule these Rebels would face. The non-conference schedule was daunting:

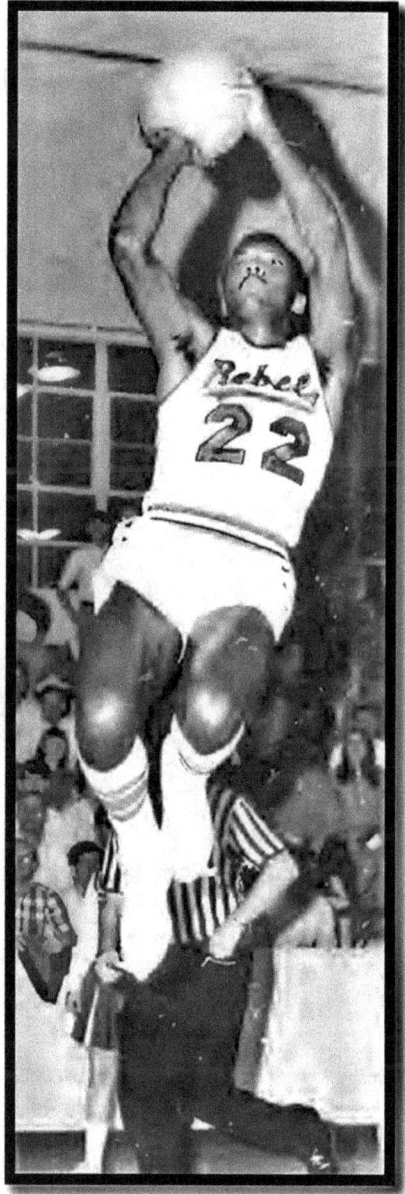

The great #22 - Pete Smith

two games each against nationally ranked FSU, rivals Georgia Southern, Oglethorpe, and the University of Tampa. The GIAC included 14 games this year, including the usual contenders, Shorter and West Georgia.

The real challenge would be the nationally ranked Berry Vikings. Before the season began, Berry was touting this squad as the best in school history. Such a schedule would be a tall task for any team, much less a team that lost five starters from last year's team.

Melvin and Dominey labored throughout the spring and summer to develop a roster that was equal to the scheduling challenge. 6-2 John Trimnell would be the sole returning player with any significant experience. Juniors Paul O'Brien, a 6-2 point guard, Dale Croft, a 6-5 post player, and sophomore Marty Lehmann at 6-4 (wing and post) were the other returning players. None of the four had ever started for the Rebels to date.

Front Row (left to right): Paul O'Brien, Lee Mahatzke, Mike Phelps, John Trimnell, Joe Brogdon. Second Row: Jimmy Dorsett, John Jones, Dale Croft, Steve Porterfield, Malcolm Lyles, Bob Suggs. Third Row: Fred Gibbons, Grayson Hurley, Marty Lehmann, Pete Smith, JW Rutledge, Coach James Dominey, Coach Jim Melvin.

To fill out the roster, Melvin and Dominey brought the following players aboard:

- 6-6 Pete Smith (Sophomore), who could play any of the five spots on the floor offensively and defensively
- 6-3 Jimmy Dorsett (Senior), who although he would only play one year at Valdosta State, was one of the great leaders and players ever to put on the uniform
- 6-7 John Jones (Junior), a JC transfer with incredible offensive skills
- 5-11 Steve Porterfield (Junior), a JC transfer point guard with stellar credentials and experience from Lake City JC in Florida
- 6-1 Joe Brogdon (Freshman), a great shooting guard from Lakeland, Georgia
- 6-2 Mike Phelps (Freshman), combo guard out of the Indianapolis area
- 6-5 Malcom Liles (Freshman), walk-on from Valdosta High School
- 6-5 Bob Suggs (Junior), a walk-on from Florida
- 6-2 JW Rutledge, a military vet who walked on

When you read "walk-on" beside a player's name, there are multiple directions your mind can go, though unfortunately, most of them negative. Not so in our realm! Within the Rebel culture, a "walk-on" is the walking definition of undaunted courage. Jim Nichols was a walk-on in Colson's second season and was instrumental in setting the Rebel Spirit tone for the program 10 years ago. Under normal circumstances, their chance of winning a starting role, much less significant time off the bench is not high; yet the players listed above showed up every day and gave everything they had at practice and encouraged their teammates during the games. They were men of character, filled with the Rebel Spirit, deserving of everyone's respect.

Armed with a roster of no returning starters, four transfers, two scholarship freshman guards, and three walk-ons, Melvin and Dominey went to work on team building, as well as installing offensive and defensive strategies. Melvin handled the offense, installing the Wheel system and an array of offensive sets versus zones. Dominey managed the defensive side of the court, which meant the Rebels would play hard-nosed, in your shirt half court man-to-man pressure defense; along with a 1-2-1-1 full-court zone press. Lehmann points out the effect this coaching tandem had on the rebuilt Rebel roster: "Coach Dominey came on and had an immediate impact with defense. Melvin and Dominey's relationship appeared seamless, they fit together perfectly. They shared the leadership, and never got into any conflict in front of us. There was a genuine respect between them, and they never got in one another's lane. It was one of the big reasons we became successful."

It is a well-known fact within Rebel lore that learning the Wheel system can be difficult for a variety of reasons. First, it is a team-based system that functions best when everyone is doing their role—setting picks, setting their man up and making the appropriate cut, making the appropriate pass, etc. There is no room for a player who is selfish, focused on individual stats in this system. The prerequisite for a player was to be unselfish and team oriented. The offense would get you a clear look at the rim. Second, you had to be patient. It might take three passes to clear someone for the shot or 10 passes. Patience wins in the clutch more often than taking a questionable shot out of impatience. Third, there were many nuances and cuts to the system, which required a player's complete attention. In summary, although the Rebels did not have any starters returning, they did have four players returning that not only understood the system but were committed to and believed in it!

The preseason practices were filled with lots of instruction and learning. Melvin and Dominey had a highly regulated schedule for practice and were expert instructors in the details on both ends of the floor. The learning curve was huge since the majority of players were new to the systems on both ends of the floor. Lehmann notes that "early on, we would have 2-3 mediocre practices followed by a great practice." Inconsistency was the early identity for the team, which is understandable at this juncture of the season.

Maty Lehmann goes high for a lay up

As the preseason wrapped up and the opener against FSU in Tallahassee approached, the coaching staff decided they would go with O'Brien at point guard, Jimmy Dorsett at the shooting guard, John Trimnell at the small forward, Pete Smith at the other forward, and John Jones at center. Joe Brogdon, Marty Lehmann, and Dale Croft would be the substitutes. A note that the substitution pattern underscored Trimnell's overall importance on both ends because he understood what everyone's role was, could play all five positions, and was the hub of communication. If O'Brien needed a rest, John could run the point. If Dorsett needed a break, Trimnell gave the coaching staff significant and necessary flexibility with a thin and relatively undersized roster.

Paul O'Brien

With the level of competition elevated, the Rebel's pre-conference record took a direct hit, hovering below .500 after New Year's. Coach Melvin discussed the struggles the Rebels had during the first half of the season, noting that "my teams historically have made significant positive steps after Christmas. My focus was always on the teaching the fundamentals and how to do them correctly, which takes time. I was confident the group of players we went into the conference schedule would respond positively."

Lehmann reflects on the impact Melvin's and Dominey's tireless belief and confidence had on the team. "The two main ingredients contributing to the success of the second half of the '68 -'69 season were leadership and chemistry. Due to the chemistry between the coaches, their providing constant encouragement and coaching, the team made an amazing transformation after the holidays. The emergence of Melvin's and Dominey's sideline leadership, as well as Jimmy Dorsett's and John Trimnell's floor leadership, made the second half of the season a magical time!"

After the holidays, as the Berry and Shorter visit to Titletown approached, the coaching staff selected the six players to fit their rotation. These six had the requisite athleticism, basketball IQ, and skills, but more importantly bought into the Rebel Way. They were team players and filled to overflowing with the Rebel Spirit—possessing uncommon levels of resilience and relentless determination required to play through the whistle! An important point is that once the decision was made to go "small", a corresponding commitment was made to use the full-court press the entirety of the game after every made basket. Dorsett, Brogdon, and O'Brien were in the frontcourt, Trimnell covered the middle, and Smith patrolled the backcourt. Lehmann came in and played whoever was throwing the ball inbounds (he was like a raging Spider Man in his effort). The press became a signature identity for this group of Rebels, who were labeled "Melvin's Midgets" by Sammy Glassman. The team speed and quickness, plus basketball instincts of Trimnell and Smith, created havoc for opposing teams from January through the remainder of the season.

It is important to note that Joe Brogdon would be only the third Rebel to start as a Freshman, following Ray McCully and Mike Terry. Lehmann would follow in the footsteps of other great 6th men: Ben Bates, Gerald Davidson, and John Trimnell. Brogdon and Dorsett were sensational shooters; their jump shots were pure "butter." Pete Smith was a mismatch with any center (including FSU's Dave Cowens) on the offensive end. When he wanted, could shut opposing centers down. (Cowens fouled out in Valdosta because he was frustrated at the treatment he received from Trimnell as well as the number of his baby hook shots that Smith blocked, stamped with "return to sender" on them!) O'Brien was a cool customer at point guard, and you would never know he had not started until this year. Trimnell was Trimnell—all he did was find a way to win!

Berry rolled into Valdosta ranked in the NAIA Top 5, bringing one of the leading scorers in the NAIA, averaging 30+ points per game. The gym was standing room only, loud, and boisterous, egged on by public address announcer, Red Cross. The Rebels came up the stairs, running onto the floor ready to play and play they did! The Rebs blasted Berry by 25+ points. Trimnell led a relentless and ferocious defensive effort by holding Berry's leading scorer to 18 points under his season average. The Rebels' full-court press, relentless pressure defense and efficient offensive execution contributed to another significant GIAC home win!

The trouncing of Berry began a run of 14 straight conference wins, sandwiched around a narrow loss to the nationally ranked FSU Seminoles in February, which saw the Rebels tied with the 'Noles with 30 seconds to go. Unfortunately, the Rebels' last shot rimmed out, allowing the Seminoles to snatch the rebound and make the free throws to eke out a narrow win over a courageous and resilient Rebel squad.

The Rebels continued their tear through the GIAC into the NAIA District 25 Tournament, where they defeated Berry (for the third time that season) in the semifinals. Their opponent in the finals, the physically powerful and proud Albany State Rams, were led by Wilbur Jones and Cowboy Ellis. Wilbur was one of eight Jones brothers who played at Albany State for Coach Rainey. Wilbur would play a number of years in the NBA. The Rams roster was loaded!

No one in the media gave the Rebels a chance against the vaunted power, speed, and talent of the Rams. The media guys forgot to check with the Rebels, who found a way to go toe-to-toe with Rams the entire game. All of those hard-fought games earlier in the season had seasoned the team and prepared them for this challenge.

The Rams' defensive strategy the last five minutes was to deny O'Brien the ball and make the rookie, Joe Brogdon, beat them. Brogdon played like a veteran guard, bringing the ball up the court in the final minutes of the game against intense man-to-man pressure, drawing foul after foul, then knocking down free throw after free throw.

The game came down to the last second (literally), with the Rebels in possession of the ball under their basket. Trimnell, as the trigger man, snapped the ball in his hands and the team ran the play as it was drawn up. It was like the Red Sea parted and Pete Smith came wide open under the basket. Trimnell looked the defender off with a glance in another direction and slipped Smith a slick no-look bounce pass. Smith went straight up and put the ball off the glass, only to have 6-9 Wilbur Jones soar across the lane to block the shot from the other side of the rim after it banked off the backboard. The official out front never hesitated, blew his whistle, and signaled goal tending! Danny Dee could be heard screaming into the WVLD radio microphone, "Rebels win! Rebels win!"

"I was confident that John Trimnell would make the right pass at the right time to the right person. It happened in an instant, the referee signaled basket good on a goal tending, I ran the length of the floor. I was thinking, wow – we did it!" Coach Melvin

The Rebels would head to Kansas City to play ninth-ranked Elizabeth City State (NC) in the first round. The Rebels stumbled out of the gates during the early morning start, getting down by 20 points at one point. As they had done throughout the second half of the year, they displayed their resilience and relentless hearts, taking the lead with less than five minutes on the clock. In the end, the Rebels ran out of gas and time; they were knocked out on this day, 86-78, by a strong team that lost in the semifinals to eventual winner Eastern New Mexico, 75-72.

Senior Jimmy Dorsett had provided incredible leadership throughout the year and averaged 13.9 ppg. Coach Melvin said of Dorsett, "he was one of the coolest players under pressure as I've ever been around. We were playing a tight game late in the season, with the clock inside of five minutes and we were out of sorts. Jimmy came by and said we needed a time out; I called the time out. Jimmy took charge in the huddle, calmed everyone down and got them refocused—which is what senior leadership is all about. In addition, he was one of the toughest defenders and rebounders we had that year." Trimnell's work ethic, absolute commitment to the team and winning were evident every night, regardless of the opponent." John's hustle play in Kansas City, when he ran half the length of the floor to chase down a loose ball—diving into the stands is still a play his teammates remember," according to Gary Colson and others on the 1966-67 team.

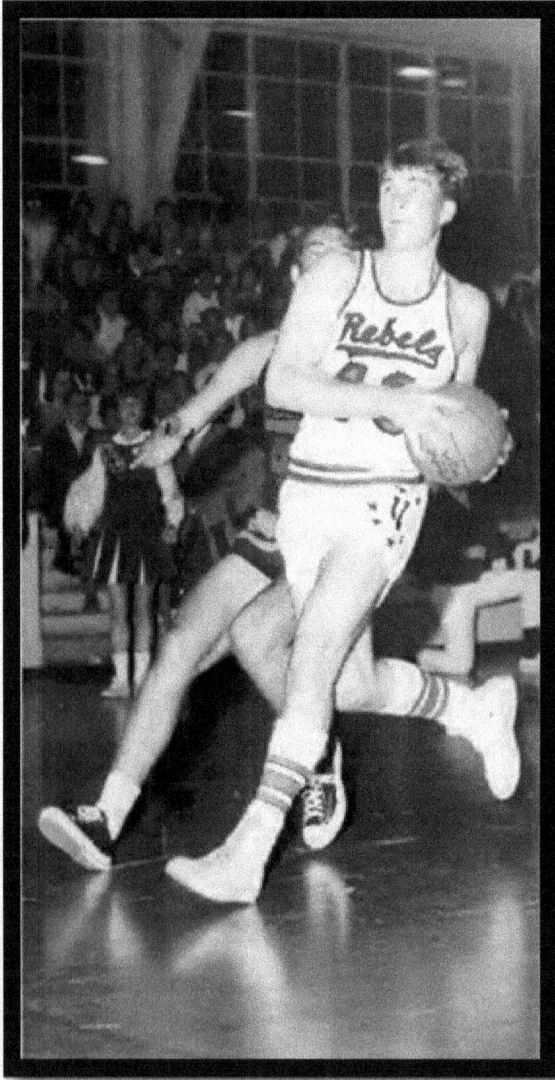

John Trimnell

Although he was not an extrovert, his actions left an indelible imprint on those around him! He was always willing to do whatever it took, including the thankless assignments. He was simply infectious; everyone caught the "willing to do what it takes" virus! (Pictured at left is Trimnell racing for a layup vs Armstrong St.)

How did Melvin's Midgets (no man in the rotation stood taller than 6-6) win a third-straight GIAC title, as well as a third-straight District 25 Championship? After all, this was supposed to be a rebuilding year according to the pundits, as well as conference and district rivals? Yet, this team, which was extremely out-manned, found a way to take third-ranked FSU to the last 10 seconds before losing, beat nationally ranked Berry College three times, and upset a powerful and highly ranked Albany State team.

In short, there are at least four keys to this great season:

1. An uncommon unity and passion forged among the team during the furnace of the early season losses. That commitment and energy empowered the Rebels to play with high levels of resilience and determination well beyond any limitations of size, numbers or experience.
2. Coaches Melvin and Dominey made incredible strategic and in-game decisions along the journey, based on the talent and soul of the team that enabled this group to continue to place another trophy in the Rebel championship legacy! Moreover, they never lost faith and confidence in the team, and provided constant instruction and encouragement. Coach Melvin was named Coach of the Year in both the GIAC and NAIA District 25.
3. The floor leadership from the Co-Captains, Senior Jimmy Dorsett and Junior John Trimnell.
4. Pete Smith. Coach Melvin said Smith was the best collegiate player in Georgia, if not the Southeast, that year. His play backed that up. His total field goal attempts (721) and rebounding average (13.7) in 68-69 are school records, and his 24.2 points per game rank 7th in Rebel history. Smith earned team MVP, GIAC MVP,

and Honorable-Mention All American honors. He was drafted by both the NBA and ABA, spending time with the ABA's San Diego Conquistadors. Smith was a pioneer on the road to integration, and because of his positive experience, more players were on the way from the Albany area to VSC in the immediate future.

The '69 Valdosta State Pine Cone summarized the team and it's accomplishments eloquently:

"Basketball is a major sport at Valdosta State. Winning basketball teams is the rule. Winning the GIAC Championship and the NAIA District Championship has become tradition. The 68-69 Rebels wrote another successful chapter. In retrospect 68-69 was perhaps VSC Basketball's finest hour. Jim Melvin and James Dominey molded a young, inexperienced squad into champions...."

GIAC Champions	District 25 Champions	NAIA Sweet 16
• 1960-61	• 1966-67	• 1966-67
• 1961-62	• 1967-68	• 1967-68
• 1962-63	• 1968-69	
• 1963-64		
• 1965-66		
• 1966-67		
• 1967-68		
• 1968-69		

VALDOSTA

10

✦

1969-70: Rising to the Challenge of Winning a 9th GIAC Championship

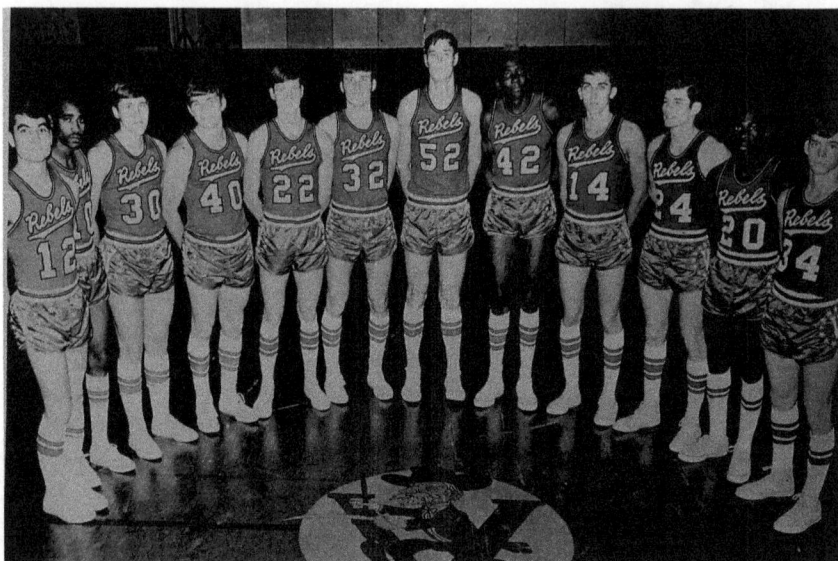

Left to right: Joe Brogdon, Willie Oxford, Roger Fleetwood, John Trimnell, Leroy Purdy, Marty Lehmann, Carlos McSwain, Robert Jones, Ashley Deloach, Paul O'Brien, Willie Yarborough, and Steve Doughty.

Coming off an unbeaten conference record of 14-0 and winning the NAIA District 25 crown the third year in a row against overwhelming odds, only served to elevate expectations for second year Head Coach Jim Melvin and his Rebels. There would be significant turnover in the roster as 50% of the primary six-man rotation was gone (Brogdon, Dorsett, and Smith). Since Rebel fans saw the results of the 1968-69 team, they were primed and ready for the 1969-70 version!

The coaching staff hit the road after Kansas City and landed some key additions that would have to make significant contributions if the Rebels were to continue their championship success. One of the key characteristics of any college coach is the ability to identify talent, at which both Melvin and Dominey were adept. In addition to talent and fit, a key objective was to develop depth and continuity from one year to the next. This recruiting class was vital to establishing a foundation for the next three to four years.

Willie Oxford and Willie Yarborough committed to the Rebels early in the spring. The dynamic guard tandem, was just what the doctor ordered to replace much of the offensive production lost from the departure of Brogdon and Smith. Then the Rebels landed Carlos McSwain, brother of Rebel great Gwendell McSwain, providing much-needed size and defensive presence in the middle, as well as being a tenacious rebounder. Then Roger Fleetwood, a 6-2 guard with Earl Monroe ball handling skills, transferred in from Indiana State. Also, 6-3 Ashley Deloach, brother of former Rebel Austin Deloach, transferred in providing depth at the forward spot. And finally, Steve Doughty, a 5-10 lightning quick and tough-nosed guard, walked on. Walk-ons Robert Jones and Leroy Purdy filled out the 1969-70 Rebel roster.

As preseason workouts began, it was clear there was a lot of team building and culture development to be done since so many new faces were in uniform. Not only did the dynamic coaching tandem recruit talented players, more importantly they selected players who fit the Rebel culture and legacy. They were players whose core values aligned with those values handed down from team to team throughout the years: uncommon levels of resiliency, hard work, passion, determination, teamwork, and a servant spirit—selfless. In short, although this team was officially born in early October '69, they coalesced quickly as a cohesive unit because they had a very uncommon passion and purpose, and were willing to do whatever it took to accomplish their objectives: a GIAC Championship and NAIA District 25 crown.

The 1969-70 schedule was loaded once again! Valdosta State had become known as a team who would take on the toughest opponents anywhere. There was no "scheduling wins," as is known in coaching circles to pad the record. Although there was no FSU this year, they were replaced by the Albany State Rams, an NAIA team loaded with talent and physical presence at every position. The Rams were scheduled to come to Valdosta early in the season. Everyone knew they would have one thing on their mind, repaying the Rebels for the loss in last year's District Final. As for talent, Albany State brought Caldwell Jones (AKA CJ), the next of the famous Jones brothers to play at Albany State. CJ was a legit 7-1, with at least a 7-foot wingspan, so he played more like 7-5. Eventually, he would become an NBA All Star with the

76ers. In addition to Albany State, the non-conference docket included small college powers Oglethorpe, Georgia Southern, and Tampa; plus Appalachian State, the University of West Florida, and a two-game road trip to Indiana where the Rebels would face teams who had been to the NAIA National Tournament.

The big game during the first month of the season was the visit from Albany State. The Rams came into the game with another boatload of talent and an attitude focused on avenging their season-ending loss last spring. This would be a heavyweight fight in every sense of the word, a big time collegiate basketball dog fight from beginning to end, with neither team being able to break the will of the other. Neither team flinched, leads were swapped, and multiple players got in foul trouble as the referees made every attempt to keep the passion and intensity under control. Foul troubles caught up with Rebels point guard Paul O'Brien late in the game, which required walk-on freshman, Steve Doughty, to play significant minutes during the three OT game. Doughty played his heart out, playing ferocious defense, as well as aggressive on the offensive end. The winner was determined in the final seconds of the third overtime when the guard from Albany State hit a 20-foot jump shot to win it at the buzzer and break the hearts of the young Rebels.

To no one's surprise, the challenge within the GIAC came from Shorter College (Rome, GA). The Hawks came into VSC's gym in early January and handed the Rebels the first home loss within the GIAC play since they turned the same trick in the District Championship game in 1965. It was the second heart-breaking loss for the Rebels this season. In addition, Georgia Southwestern gave the Rebels another surprising conference loss in February in Americus. This edition of the Rebels had consistently been able to bounce back because of that uncommon resilience from deep within the team. Consequently, they would go on to win the next six conference games to set up a winner-take-all game at Shorter late in February, which saw the Rebels play lights out, beating Shorter by 15 points to win the GIAC conference outright.

Late in the season, the Rebels had a rematch at Albany State. The

Rebels hammered the Rams by 17 points in their most convincing victory of the season. The Rebels literally controlled every aspect of the game from beginning to end. The young team was maturing as the season wound toward tournament time.

The Rebels were off to their fifth-straight NAIA District 25, this time in Augusta. As the basketball gods would have it, their semifinal opponent would come from the GIAC again, Shorter College. The Rebs dispatched Shorter a second time within the span of three weeks in a tight, 2-point contest. Joining VSC in the finals was an experienced, physically imposing and highly ranked group from Augusta College. The home court advantage proved too much for the Rebels to overcome, with Augusta winning a hard-fought contest, 60-54.

The Rebels season ended with a 19-11 record, another GIAC Championship (12-2), the ninth in the last 10 years, and a fifth-straight trip to the NAIA District 25 Tournament. The Rebels were led by senior co-captains John Trimnell and Paul O'Brien.

Trimnell, a three-year letterman, had an outstanding senior season. He was Honorable Mention All American, NAIA District 25 All-Star Team, and GIAC All-Conference. He was the galvanizing force within the Rebels' relentless defense, always taking the toughest defensive assignment night in and night out. Although he was 6-2 he rebounded like a 6-7 demon on the boards on both ends of the floor. Trimnell was steady on offense, always willing to serve a complementary role throughout his career, scoring 881 points.

O'Brien was the field general, consistently taking care of the ball and getting the Rebels into positions where they could be successful, as well as being a sinewy strong and hard-nosed defender. He shot 53% from the floor for his career. His role required an uncommon amount of discipline, selflessness, and humility, since his job was to get other players in positions to score.

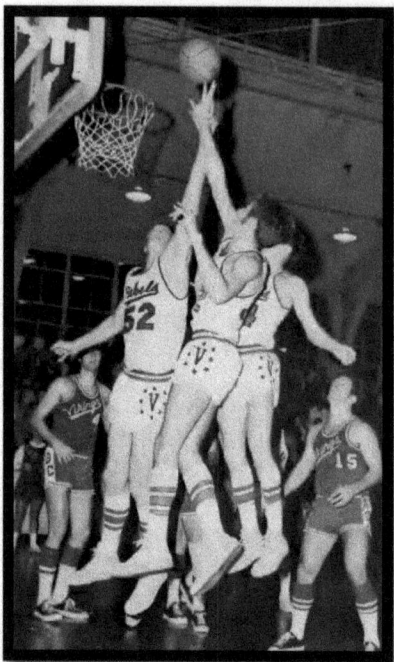

McSwain (52) reaches for a rebound

When Joe Brogdon transferred to UGA, it became obvious that Dawson's Willie Oxford would have to get acclimated quickly to the collegiate game for the Rebels offense to be effective and productive. Oxford stepped into a starting role (only the fourth freshman to do so) and never missed a beat! He demonstrated a silky-smooth offensive game complemented by a level of intensity on the defensive end and re-bounding that belied his slender 6-2 frame. Oxford stepped right into those shooting guard's shoes and averaged 16.8 points per game for the Rebels, scoring 505 points during the season. He was named GIAC All Conference for his efforts!

In summary, there were a number positive takeaways from the 1969-70 edition of the Valdosta State Rebels:

- The Albany area connection (Pete Smith, Willie Oxford and Willie Yarborough) had paid huge dividends for Coach Melvin's Rebels over his first two seasons.

- Willie Oxford's play as a freshman provided a glimpse of what the next three years might look like with this silky smooth, ultra-competitive Rebel.
- The objective to develop depth took a big step forward; returning for the 1970-71 edition would be Lehmann, Deloach, Oxford, Fleetwood, Yarborough, and Doughty. All had played significant roles at various times during the season.
- Winning the GIAC for the ninth time in 10 years.
- Making an unprecedented fifth-consecutive trip to the NAIA District 25 Tournament.

Trimnell drives against Southwestern

There is one thing as sure as the sun rises in the East when you talk to anyone from Valdosta regarding either football or basketball: Championships are what count. Expectations were more elevated than ever before; therefore, much work had to be done with the returning players and bringing in another set of recruits that could not only play but fit the Rebel culture. The dynamic duo (Melvin and Dominey) of young coaches in Georgia and the Southeast were ready for the challenge and hit the road in search of a "few good men" as they closed the books on 1969-70 and focused on the next decade's first squad.

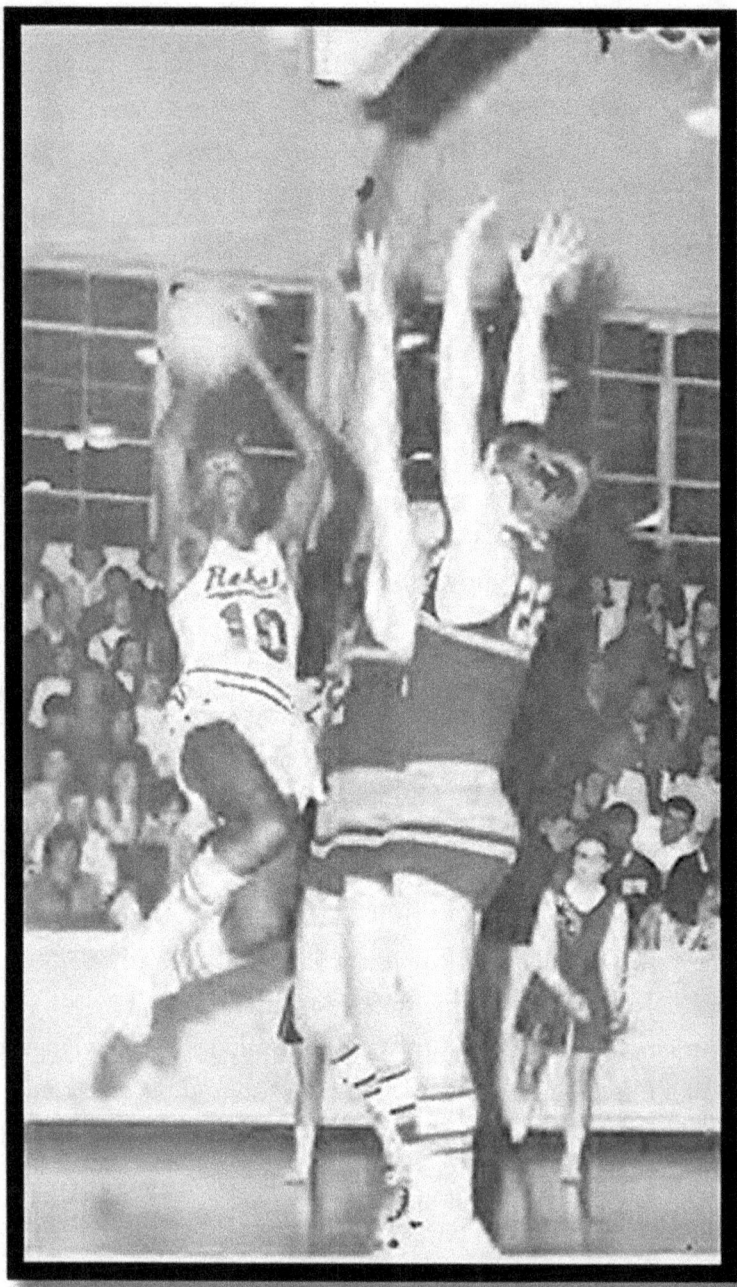

Willie Oxford goes in for a score.

1970-71 New Decade - Same Results

1970-71: New Decade, Same Results – the Rebels' 10ᵗʰ GIAC Championship!

Jim Melvin's third edition of the Rebels embraced championship aspirations just as each of the previous squads in the 60s had—winning the GIAC and competing for the NAIA District 25 crown.

The roster in this edition of the Rebels was anchored by four returning lettermen: Marty Lehmann, Willie Oxford, Roger Fleetwood, and Willie Yarborough. Lehmann and Oxford were the two leading scorers from last year's team. Lehmann was the 6th man two years ago, who was a ball of fire and energy when he came onto the floor. Roger Fleetwood assumed that role last year, as Lehmann became a starter. If there was ever a fit for a player within the Rebel culture, Fleetwood was it. If you had seen John Havlicek play the 6th man role for the 1960's Boston Celtics, then you know the definition of the 6th man: determination, heart, hustle, selflessness, and a relentless pursuit of excellence. Fleetwood was the epitome of the 6th man within Rebel culture and lore!

Otherwise, the roster would contain new arrivals of talent, size, and culture fit. It took a special person to earn a roster spot at Valdosta State and to follow in the championship footsteps of players like Melvin, Nichols, McCulley, Ritch, Terry, Fortner, Perry, McSwain, Phillips, Lamphier, Trimnell, O'Brien, among others. Although it required talent and ability, more importantly it required character and attitude. The players that fit the Rebel culture had uncommon levels of passion, perseverance, and purpose in the pursuit of excellence—in the face of challenge and adversity, as well as an elevated level of resilience (bounce back quotient) and self-confidence. In addition, they must demonstrate a marked selflessness on both ends of the floor and a commitment to teamwork seldom found either then or today.

"I was not initially recruited by Valdosta State. Coach Dominey was at a game observing another player from Jasper (FL). One of the officials told him they needed to take a look at this kid from P. K. Yonge HS, Jim Springfield. After checking me out, they liked my game and potential, invited me to a tryout. I loved Valdosta, which was a lot like Gainesville at that time. Coach Melvin was inspirational in the way he approached life and the game, which made the choice easy for me."

Jim Springfield

These characteristics would be demonstrated over and over on the defensive end, whether it meant taking the other team's number one player, defending, and shutting down someone 4- to 6-inches taller, or helping offside to close the driving lanes. In short, Rebel players were known to be ferociously competitive, committed to doing whatever it took to win possessions, to win games and eventually, championships. Playing through the echo of the whistle!

Left to Right: Donnie Wisenbaker, Willie Oxford, Roger Fleetwood, Tommy Prichard, Jimmy Edwards, Bob Donohoe, Jim Springfield, Greg Lee, Marty Lehman, Tim Dominey, Pete Lahey, Willie Yarbrough.

One year ago, Fleetwood and Oxford came aboard, making incredible contributions—albeit in different roles, making it clear they would be cornerstones for years to come in the backcourt. This year's recruiting class was another step forward in developing talent, depth, and recruiting pipelines:

- Eric Mance, a prized 6-4 swing man, committed to the Rebels. The strong and talented player from Albany could play outside or inside.
- Tim Dominey, a 6-2 combo guard out of Vienna by way of ABAC was a great shooter from deep, as well as a solid ball handler who would be asked to fill in the point guard spot vacated by Paul O'Brien's graduation.
- The frontcourt needed help, since Lehmann was the only player left. Help came in the form of 1) Jim Springfield, a talented 6-6, 225-pound power forward from Gainesville, FL. 2) Bob Donohue, a 6-9, 250-pound center from Atlanta who could knock down the 18-20-foot jump shot from the top of the key that had become a staple of the Wheel Offense. 3) Tommy Pritchard, a 6-5, 190-pound swing whose toughness was belied by his slender frame. 4) Jimmy Edwards, a 6-8, 200-pound forward/center, who had the ability to knock down 15-16 footers. 5) Greg Lee, a 6-4,

200-pound forward, joined the Rebels after his tour of duty concluded in the military.

- Donnie Wisenbaker, a sensational guard out of Dasher, just down the road from VSC, was the only pure point guard recruit. Wisenbaker had been a point guard by position, but his shot-making ability made many observers wonder if he would be better at the two guard spot. The Rebels were counting on him helping firm up the point guard position, though.

As preseason workouts began, it was clear there was more depth across the board than when Coach Melvin started his coaching journey three years ago, when the Rebels used what amounted to a five-guard lineup in 1968-69. This Rebel squad appeared, at least on paper, that they had all the essential earmarks to embark successfully on the new campaign: talent, size, and most important of all, they fit the mold of the Rebel culture.

A couple of interesting and critical events occurred during fall workouts. First, Mance injured his knee and would be lost for the season. Although this was not a career-ending injury, Mance's loss would be significant due to his talent, size, and strength. Second, the players elected Lehmann and Gibbons co-captains. Lehmann had earned everyone's respect and admiration over his career, epitomizing what a Rebel player should be. Gibbons, on the other hand, had been the manager and trainer recruited by Coach Melvin in '68. This tandem of Senior leaders, one on the floor and the other from the sideline, were two-thirds of the "glue" (along with Roger Fleetwood) that effectively facilitated the development of a cohesive and unified locker room. These leaders represented the Rebel spirit—that never-say-die attitude, from which the other team members drew motivation and inspiration of what it meant to wear the Rebel uniform. Their uncommon levels of passion, selflessness, and resilience would be tested severely this year since there would be plenty of challenges and adversity, beginning with the schedule!

The 1970-71 schedule was loaded ... again! Valdosta State continued to take on the toughest opponents. FSU returned to the schedule this year, and although Dave Cowens had graduated, the Seminoles would end up playing for the National Championship in the spring. Next up was another nationally ranked power, the Jacksonville University Dolphins. The Dolphins were loaded, including Chipley, Florida's 7-3 Artis Gilmore and 7-footer Pembrook Burrows. Then there were two games each with the Albany State Rams (Caldwell Jones), Oglethorpe, Georgia Southern, and Tampa. In addition, the Rebels were scheduled to play a tournament in Columbus, GA, where they would face two nationally ranked small colleges: Georgetown College (KY) and Columbus College (which would become VSC's District 25 rival this season).

In Melvin's three years, during the regular season, the Rebels had faced the following future NBA players: Dave Cowens (Celtics), Caldwell Jones (76ers), Artis Gilmore (Bulls), and Foots Walker (Cavaliers). Hugh Durham had the FSU Seminoles on a roll, headed toward a showdown with UCLA for a national championship. Joe Williams had Jacksonville University headed on a similar trajectory. Albany State kept bringing in the next Jones' brother (there were eight of them who played at Albany State), plus a cast of exceptional players. There is a long-lasting Rebel principle: You've got to play and beat the best to be the best!

There were multiple big games early in the season. Out of the chute, the Rebels tangled with Albany State, dispatching them at home by 2 points. That was followed by a narrow win over GIAC foe, Piedmont College in Valdosta. The Rebels lost two road games in this stretch, to Tampa and FSU. They bounced back to

Roger Fleetwood and Tim Dominey celebrate in the locker room after a big win

defeat archrival Oglethorpe in Atlanta by 1 point. Then trips to Albany State and Georgia Southern brought two more losses. The fall campaign ended with the tournament in Columbus, where the Rebels defeated a strong Georgetown College (KY) team by 10 points in the semifinals and lost to the home team, Columbus College, in a 107-104 shootout. The record stood at 4-5 as the Rebels closed out 1970 and focused on winning another GIAC title.

The challenge within the GIAC came from multiple teams this season: Piedmont, LaGrange, West Georgia, and pesky Georgia Southwestern. The Rebels had already played an uncharacteristically early conference game in November, defeating a surprisingly tough Piedmont squad by two points. When the winter schedule began, the Rebels reeled off three-straight conference wins, the last of which was a dramatic 3-point victory over West Georgia in Valdosta. Marty Lehmann's dunk over Foots Walker with only seconds left was as ferocious a dunk in a hotly contested game as anyone had seen! The GIAC record stood at 4-0.

Then Georgia Southwestern played spoilers again, defeating the Rebels by holding them to 53 points. Piedmont won a shootout 101-92 in Demorest, before the Rebels righted the ship and season by winning five conference games in a row. In that run, the Rebs beat West Georgia at Carrollton 80-50, and LaGrange two times in two weeks. The 1-point win in LaGrange came as a result of Willie Oxford's 14 free throws, which still remains tied for the most FT in a game by a Valdosta State player. The Rebs' conference mark stood at 9-2, with only Georgia Southwestern left at Valdosta. GSW came in and stole a 72-71 victory. Although the Rebels ended up winning the GIAC, there was sour taste in everyone's heart.

The latter half of the schedule included four games against non-conference Oglethorpe, Tampa, Georgia Southern, and Jacksonville University's Homecoming game on regional TV. The Rebels beat Oglethorpe, sweeping the season series for the first time in years. Next up, the Tampa Spartans, coached by Dana Kirk who was headed to Memphis State after the season. The Rebels beat them handily by 17 points in front of a packed house at Valdosta. The Jacksonville Dolphins would be the tallest team Coach Melvin's Rebels faced in his tenure. The JU lineup was 5-11, 6-8, 6-10, 7, and 7-3. Although the Rebels found a way to stay with the Dolphins throughout the first half, the second half found the Rebels unable to hit key jump shots, and the Dolphins won by 22 points. Last up was a tussle with District 25 rival, Georgia Southern, at Valdosta.

The Eagles had had their way with the Rebels for some time. This would be the last home game for senior co-captains Lehmann and Gibbons, and surprisingly for Head Coach Jim Melvin. Coach announced his resignation prior to the game. Over the years, Coach Melvin explained this choice was the result of much thought and prayer, and aspirational in nature. He recently said, "I loved coaching, and coaching in Valdosta. I would never have coached anywhere else. With that said, I had scratched that itch and there was another itch I needed to explore, educational leadership." Consequently, the emotion and intensity were ratcheted up because every player and staff loved and respected Coach Melvin. There was no way the Georgia Southern Eagles were going to ruin this going away party! The crowd was standing room only, revved up when legendary public address announcer Red Cross went into his crowd-charging player and staff introductions, to the point the hair on the back of our necks was standing up! The energy on the floor within the team and noise from the crowd never waned, and the Rebs beat the Eagles, 75-67, in a fiercely fought contest.

The Rebels were off to their sixth-straight NAIA District 25, this time in Columbus, where the Rebs had dropped a 3-point shootout 107-104 in December. The Rebs were the fourth seed in the District Tournament primarily because of the two losses to GSW. That meant they would play top-seeded Columbus, which looked and played eerily like Augusta in last year's District Tournament. They were experienced, physically imposing, and highly ranked, and playing at home. Columbus proved to be the better team that night, beating the Rebels, 86-77.

The Rebels' season ended with a 15-10 record, another GIAC Championship (9-3) the 10th in the last 11 years, and a sixth-straight trip to the NAIA District 25 Tournament.

There were a number of positive takeaways from the 1970-71 edition of the Valdosta State Rebels:

- The team stood shoulder to shoulder, unified, throughout the season! The theme seemed to be "three steps forward, two steps back," which is not surprising with the number of new faces on the team. There were moments when the Rebels were invincible, then moments when other teams played at a level (and/or with more talent) that exposed the inexperience in the squad.
- The Albany-Dawson Pipeline rolled on (Pete Smith, Willie Oxford, and Willie Yarborough) with the addition of Eric Mance. This recruiting pipeline paid huge dividends for Coach Melvin's Rebels, enhancing the talent, character, and depth on the team. The pipeline would continue to produce great ball players in the near future for the Rebels.
- Willie Oxford's play as a sophomore served to begin the conversation of his status as one of the best guards ever to wear a Rebel uniform.
- In the frontcourt, although Lehmann was leaving, there were ample numbers of talented players in every slot returning next year. The Rebel coaching staff had built some much needed depth up and down the lineup.
- Splitting with non-conference rivals Albany St., Tampa, and Georgia Southern, and sweeping Oglethorpe was a significant step forward.
- Winning the GIAC for the 10th time in the conference's 11 years is a significant accomplishment in any league at any level.
- Making an unprecedented sixth consecutive trip to the NAIA District 25 Tournament.

The role of team captains is critical in any sport. Captains are the internal team alchemist, the glue that fuses a disparate group of players together around a common set of values; inspiring and motivating the team toward objectives that otherwise could not be attained. The Rebels historically had incredible captains and this season was no different. Senior co-captains Marty Lehmann and Fred Gibbons are pictured below.

Lehmann, a three-year letterman, had an outstanding senior season. He was GIAC All Conference. He was the galvanizing force within the Rebels' relentless defense, always taking the toughest defensive assignment night in and night out. Although he was 6-4, he rebounded like he was 6-7. His dunk over Foots Walker in Valdosta is legendary! As he matured as a player, his offensive game soared, averaging double figures his last two years. Lehmann's extraordinary never-say-die energy and determination inspired his teammates. He was selfless to a fault, willing to take the assignment or role no one else wanted.

1970-71 REBEL CAPTAINS
Marty Lehmann, left, a 6-3 senior from Griffith, Ind., and Fred Gibbons, senior trainer from Tampa, Fla., were elected by team members to captain this year's team. Both young men are outstanding leaders. Lehmann has been a starter for two seasons, and Gibbons was winner of the "Rebel Spirit" award each of the past two years.

Although Gibbons never scored a point, snatched a rebound or recorded a steal, he more than personified the Rebel Spirit. Gibbons contracted polio in 1953 at the age of five and would never run again, wearing a full-length brace on his left leg (except during practice when he would go without the brace). His unending enthusiasm, encouragement, and positive outlook from the sidelines and training room was a rich resource the team drew on, but never more important than when the circumstances looked the bleakest. Gibbons learned through his rehab (learning how to walk with braces) that no matter how many times you fall, you can get back up and take another step—a daily example of Vince Lombardi's "it's not whether or not you get knocked down by adversity, but whether you decide to get back up." Gibbons' uncommon resilience, selflessness, and positive outlook is the essence of what he brought to the team and was truly humbled to win the Rebel Spirit Award every year he was a Rebel ('68, '69, and '70).

If Rebel fans thought Oxford's freshman campaign was special, when he averaged 16.8 points and scored 505 points, his encore act was simply extraordinary, even magical at times. In his sophomore year, he averaged 19.9 points per game and scored 499 points, which meant Oxford joined the 1,000 career point club as a sophomore (having played just 55 games). His poise under extreme duress and pressure was remarkable, as every team was aware of and trying to shut him down. No more so than when he shot and made 14 free throws to clinch the game at LaGrange or his teardrop over Artis Gilmore in the lane in Jacksonville. Oxford was named GIAC All Conference for the second year in a row!

Another standout was Tim Dominey, who proved to be the perfect complement to Oxford at guard. Dominey was an excellent shooter and ball handler, amazingly effective at either the point or shooting guard. He averaged 13.3 points per game and scored 306 points in his first campaign as a Rebel. Consequently, the Rebels' backcourt was set for the next couple of years with All-Conference players.

Roger Fleetwood's role as 6th man cannot be understated. His burst of high intensity effort and execution (regardless of the role he was filling) when he hit the floor super-charged the team. His basketball IQ was off the charts, and he was looked at as a coach on the floor throughout his career. He was completely selfless, although fully capable of knocking down crucial shots. He was a major "influencer" on the floor and in the locker room. Mike Krzyzewski, Duke Head Coach, says that after talent, the most important ingredient he looks for in recruits is their leadership ability to set and demonstrate higher standards among their teammates. Once again, the recruiting ability of this coaching staff had selected a player who personified the Rebel Spirit.

Jim Melvin's Accomplishments and Legacy

Coach Melvin stepped down as head coach to pursue an Ed.D. in Educational Leadership at the University of Georgia. He had been a fixture within the Rebel program for seven years; two years as a player ('59-'60), two years as an Assistant Coach, and three years as a Head Coach. He had left an indelible fingerprint and legacy on the Rebel program.

- Coach Melvin not only maintained the continuity of the championship culture Gary Colson had established but enhanced it. Under Melvin's leadership, the Rebels recorded 52 wins against 32 losses (61.9%), three GIAC Championships (33-5, 87%), three trips to the NAIA District 25 Tournament, and one trip to the NAIA National Championship in Kansas City. In 1968-69, led by the dynamic coaching duo of Melvin and Dominey, the Rebels never missed a beat, immediately capturing "lightning in a bottle" and going undefeated in the GIAC. Another amazing fact was the 1968-69 Rebels, "Melvin's Midgets," went undefeated starting five guards and was only the third team in GIAC history to go undefeated. (Melvin was the point guard on the '60 team that went undefeated.) Coach Melvin's philosophy focused on "executing fundamentals correctly, but more importantly" on constant praise and encouragement of the team regardless of the circumstances. He embraced adversity by emphasizing how to use it to learn from, whether it was a loss or a turnover during a game. Consequently, the team embraced adversity and it became a strand within the Rebel Spirit DNA. He said, "adversity are the steps you climb on to get to another mountaintop," which is very similar in spirit of this quote from Abigail Adams to her son, John Quincy Adams, in the midst of the American Revolution, "It is not in the still calm of life, or the repose of a pacific station, that great characters are formed, ... the habits of a vigorous mind are formed in contending with difficulties. Great necessities call out great virtues."

• The test of whether or not a team is a dynasty is "can you dominate your peers for a decade or more?" Over the past 11 years (including Melvin's three teams, along with two as Assistant and two as a player) the Rebels answered that question with an emphatic yes! Yet the next test of any dynastic organization, athletic or otherwise, is what happens when there is a change at the top? It is extremely unusual for programs at any level to lose the head coach who was the transformational catalyst and maintain their championship ways. The Rebel Championship Dynasty remained intact! Bill Parcells said, "you are what your record says you are." In the Rebels' case, they were a dynasty within the GIAC.

• If Colson was the catalytic spark of "turn around leadership" at VSC, Melvin was the transformational leadership bridge to the 70s, and into the 21st century! Jim Melvin hired James Dominey, which affected the next 38 years of Valdosta Basketball and Athletics. In doing so, Melvin practiced what Doris Kearns Goodwin describes in her recent book, *Leadership in Turbulent Times*, by creating a team of diverse leaders. Kearns Goodwin explains that "when you're building a team, one of the most important things is to know where your own weaknesses are and what strengths you need to complement those weaknesses. What experiences are you lacking, and what experiences can you bring into the team?" She emphasizes the importance of having the confidence to not feel threatened by people who will argue with you, challenge your assumptions, and debate what is going on rather than echoing like-minded ideas. Nick Saban hires assistants who are qualified to be head coaches based upon the same logic. Why? He knows that the players and program will be better! Coach Melvin clearly has many leadership talents and skills, among them the ability to identify talent and culture fit is right at the top! By hiring someone who would prove to be a great head coach in his own right, Melvin demonstrated a high level of confidence, courage, humility, and wisdom. Dominey's hiring created one of the great coaching staffs of that era and was a cornerstone decision that long affected VSC basketball!

- A third Melvin legacy was his ability and willingness to model both servant and shared leadership. Melvin practiced servant leadership every day, regardless of with whom he was interacting. He spoke with respect and actively listened to others. Again, his genuine respect for others and humility stands out in his ability to connect with players, staff, administrators, and fans. Ashley Deloach remembers asking to speak with Coach Melvin after practice during the 1969-70 season and Coach Melvin going with him to the classroom in the basement, then listening intently to Ashley as he described the issues he was having with his back that prevented him from playing like he wanted. Melvin's response was empathetic and practical, "take care of yourself, we will be alright." Deloach remembers the conversation to this day because of Melvin's empathy and compassion for him. One of his best friends in life, Mike Perry, describes this servant spirit on the floor, explaining "Jim would rather pass the ball to a teammate to score than shoot it himself." To this day, Jim Melvin would do what he could to serve his former teammates or players. At the same time, there was no doubt who the head coach was, although he preferred to share the leadership with Dominey. The two coaches complemented one another in personalities and respective leadership/management styles. Yet, their core values and team aspirations were similar and aligned with the Rebel culture. It was clear they were united in their strategic vision and plan, going about executing it from day one, i.e., developing a recruiting pipeline, recruiting talent along with fit, and building depth in order to enhance continuity from year to year. Their game plans were clear and concise, carefully capitalizing on the respective team's strengths. Their communication with the team and individuals made clear what the expectations were and that they thought the player (and team) could meet or exceed those. There was affirmation and positive encouragement to the players, even when corrective and constructive feedback was necessary.

• Melvin's legacy is also linked to the success players had after graduating. His aspirational leadership became entrenched within the Rebel DNA over his tenure; striving for perfection while realizing you would find excellence along the way became a way of looking at opponents and life. Playing an incredibly loaded non-conference schedule is not usually a way for coaches to remain employed. Most coaches use non-conference games to add wins—not Coach Melvin. More importantly, when he resigned, it was because of an aspirational objective— moving into executive leadership of educational systems. Melvin became one of the leading school superintendents in the U.S. "After the initial reaction and having time to think about it, I realized his resignation was a great example to all of us! Through his decision to step away from the game and school he loved to move onto a bigger game outside the lines, we learned what true courage and confidence associated with aspirational thinking looks like in real life. He was saying there was a lot of life outside the doors of the gym that we could significantly positively affect! From this example, we learned that life is made up of a number of chapters, that this was not the beginning of the end but the end of the beginning." His players became world-class leaders in education, agribusiness, business, ministry, finance, and athletics; successfully negotiating the turbulent changes that occurred over the last 50 years in our country.

• Perhaps the most significant accomplishment and legacy of the Jim Melvin era was the seamless manner with which the integration of athletics occurred at Valdosta State. By managing this sensitive, but important, action in such a direct, yet compassionate manner, he won the confidence of the team and fans. It was Coach Melvin's genuine and personable nature that created trust within black coaches and players in South Georgia, of which Pete Smith was the first player. Others in the next 2-3 years were Willie Oxford, Willie Yarborough, Robert Jones, Kenny Alston, and Eric Mance. Melvin was a trusted leader of men by high school coaches in South Georgia.

The acid test of championship cultures is what happens when there is more change at the top, in this case Coach Melvin stepping down after three years? The Rebels' championship culture was facing the headwinds of change in executive leadership for the second time in three years. Dr. Martin, as he did with naming Jim Melvin Head Coach quickly, named James Dominey the Head Coach in short order. Dr. Martin's swift action (as well as the confidence the players, staff, and fans had gained in Dominey) filled the culture with confidence rather than uncertainty! Everyone connected was assured that the continuity of the Rebel Spirt and championship culture would not fade, but only shine brighter under Dominey's leadership!

12

⚜

The Dominey Years: An Uncommon Commitment to Excellence Over the Long Haul

Introduction

If there was ever going to be a test of organizational culture, a second head coaching change within three years would provide just such a challenge. The Rebel culture would face this challenge with someone who came aboard three years earlier as a 26-year-old assistant, James Dominey. Coach Dominey arrived in 1968 with an excellent pedigree of basketball experience and knowledge, more importantly with the character that fit Titletown like a hand in the glove!

Coach Dominey is from Vienna, Georgia, where he was a standout player for the legendary high school coach, Glenn Cassell, then starred at Norman JC. Next, he played for Garland Pinholster at Oglethorpe, and worked as a graduate assistant at Middle Tennessee State under

Ken Trickey. His first head coaching job was at Dykes High School, where he was spotted by Coach Melvin.

Coach Dominey had been offered the Dykes HS job after completing grad school at Middle Tennessee State. At the conclusion of the interview, the AD offered Dominey the job and this caveat: "If you win four games with this group, you'll be considered a miracle worker." Dykes was in Atlanta, playing within the largest classification in HS athletics in the state— where the competition was not for the faint of heart. The Dykes AD found the right coach! Someone who loved a challenge and, although short on coaching experience, knew how to bring the best out of the talent around him! Dykes went 10-8, so Coach Dominey was much more than the miracle worker the Dykes' AD had been seeking.

Jim Melvin was in Atlanta in the spring of 1968, at the end of the high school season, when he decided to visit and scout Dykes HS. Up to this point, he did not know Coach Dominey personally nor had he seen him coach or play. Coach Melvin explained what attracted him to Coach Dominey: "His Dykes team was outmanned but not outcoached! They were hard-nosed scrappers, who played fundamentally sound on both ends of the court. I could tell

Coach James Dominey at the beginning of his multi-decade tenure.

James had sculpted them into a ferociously competitive group that were finding ways to win. I knew the Valdosta State job was more than likely going to be offered to me. After watching his squad compete and James' demeanor from the sidelines, I felt James and I would make a great tandem." In Coach Melvin's mind, the interview was over. He had seen the "proof in the pudding" in a matter of speaking! Coach Melvin hopefully had a key piece of the culture puzzle, an assistant coach who complemented his style, knowledge, and experience; more importantly, he had core beliefs and values that aligned with the Rebel DNA.

Coach Dominey picks up the story: "After the game, Coach Melvin introduced himself, explained the situation that might happen at Valdosta State, and wanted to know if I would be interested in being his assistant. I was somewhat startled, but honored, and said sure. We left it at that, and I had not given it much thought when a couple of weeks later, Coach Melvin called. 'I guess you know why I'm calling, are you ready to come to Valdosta?' Monica and I moved to Valdosta shortly after that."

One of the overarching critical executive leadership skills is hiring the people with the requisite skills and temperament that fit with the culture, staff, and other leaders. Colson hired Melvin, and now Melvin hires Dominey! Although all three men have different personalities and coaching styles, they are aligned at the core belief and value level—hard work, integrity, transparency, loyalty, trust, teamwork, competitive, innovative, resilient, relentless, and visionary. Continuity and consistency within the Rebel Basketball culture was ensured!

Dominey says he loved working with Jim Melvin. Why? They practiced shared leadership—Melvin coordinated the offense and Dominey coordinated the defense—thus the moniker, Dominey Defense. "He demonstrated a high level of trust in me, which in turn meant a lot to my confidence as a coach and person. I had to live up to that trust and respect!" Coach Dominey said "we expected to win the GIAC, that's what Valdosta did! We were confident in our ability to put together a plan to win that capitalized on the player's abilities and attitudes, and we did." More importantly, Dominey pointed out that in the three years they worked together, there was never a time when a high level of conflict arose between them, which he felt the players recognized because not once did any player try to play both ends against the middle with them. The level of trust and respect between the two leaders set the tone for the players!

Dominey was familiar with VSC and their championship tradition since he played for Oglethorpe. More importantly, he was intimately familiar with the infamous wheel offense the Rebels ran because he played for the originator of the offense, Oglethorpe's Garland Pinholster. Dominey explains that many of his former Oglethorpe teammates questioned "why he would work for a rival?" It is important to remember that Pinholster and Colson's philosophy and styles were remarkably similar, so Dominey was steeped in what it took to win championships at every level in his history as a player. The transition from Atlanta to Valdosta State would be seamless for him. His core beliefs, values, and philosophy fit the Rebel culture to a "T!"

A key element of Coach Dominey's leadership philosophy was simple, but effective: remain true to who he was and walk the talk, i.e., personal integrity. Integrity to Coach Dominey meant living up to a high bar of excellence in every facet of life. His leadership philosophy and coaching style originated from his past coaches, specifically his high school coach. Coach Dominey said that what impressed him about his high school coach was that he walked the talk.

"He helped us understand that what we ate and drank became fuel, that Coca-Colas weren't a healthy way to get into and stay in shape. We pull up to his house one day and he's on the porch eating an apple, just like he asked us to do." A leader's willingness and ability to align their behavior with their leadership message is the hallmark of an effective leader's integrity. This core belief and value was the foundational element of Dominey's relationship with his players, staff, and university administrators. His players trust him to this day for those reasons! He was loyal to staff and players while they were an active part of the Valdosta State basketball culture and after they left.

Dominey's leadership style included being direct with expectations and feedback. You never had to wonder what he wanted or expected or where you stood. While his feedback and instruction were straightforward, players never felt belittled. Just the opposite, they felt challenged, equipped, and empowered to play at a higher level, regardless of the odds stacked against them.

Coach Dominey was an incredible strategic and tactical coach, especially when it came to teaching players how to play "Dominey Defense" —half-court, in-your-face, relentless man-to-man pressure with help coming from the back side. "You had to be mentally, emotionally, and physically tough to play Dominey Defense the entire game," according to Bob Lamphier, who served on Dominey's staff in the early 70s. Coach Dominey believed in "relentless pressure defense, whether it was in the full-court press or half court man-to-man," says Marty Lehmann. He expected everyone to "put the glove" (shut them down) on the man they were assigned to defending. He was an excellent teacher of the fine points of the game, helping everyone understand the smallest details such as cutting off angles to deny dribble penetration or the passing lanes. When he stepped in to demonstrate a technique, he did it full throttle, providing a clear example of the technique and the requisite intensity. Players were tuned in because Coach Dominey's lessons were taught with an uncommon passion and enthusiasm.

He led and coached by setting high expectations for himself as well as others, then letting his work ethic and attention to detail set the tone for the staff and team. His expectations did not stop at "putting the glove" on your assignment but also translated in a tough schedule. The Rebels were not known for dodging a great matchup and that tradition carried forward with James Dominey. The bigger the team and matchup, the more elevated his level of detail went, making every effort to turn over every stone into an opportunity for his team to be successful. While you may not describe him as obsessed with planning and preparation, he was extremely thorough, the epitome of "when you prepare for everything, you're ready for anything." Marty Lehmann shared that Dominey "set the bar high for himself and the team; the team followed his lead." In short, he expected everyone associated with the team to strive for perfection in every area of life.

His leadership style included a very polished professional persona all the way down to the polished shoes. Coach Dominey was the epitome of "professional" from his appearance at practice and games, to the written and verbal communication with fans, administrators, officials, and the media. He was poised and able to manage the emotional peaks and valleys within games with incredible balance and calm, which meant his team could play free of peeking over their shoulders out of fear. Fred Gibbons remarked that, "He handled himself with honor and respect, whether we won or lost, although I know inside, he was torn up with a loss. Coach Dominey showed me what it was to be the consummate champion, regardless of the circumstance." Bill Walsh believed that leadership was about the example you set: "Others follow you based on the quality of your actions rather than the magnitude of your declarations." Walsh's quote describes James Dominey in a nutshell.

The 1971-72 season would prove that there was continuity within Rebel basketball, as the Rebels captured their 11th GIAC title in 12 seasons during Dominey's first campaign as head coach. It would be the Rebels' last GIAC Championship, since the school moved toward NCAA membership the next season. Coach Dominey's teams remained successful throughout his 29-year head coaching career at Valdosta State, where he retired as the winningest head coach in Valdosta State history with 436 career victories. Dominey led VSC to conference championships in 1972, 1977, 1979, 1980, and 1981; to national tournament appearances on three occasions and counted 20 winning seasons among his 29.

During his tenure as head coach, his steady, disciplined, and passionate leadership guided the basketball program through changes: 1) in branding from the Rebels to the Blazers (1973), 2) in conference affiliations multiple times, and 3) the introduction of intercollegiate football to the athletic programs and the ensuing step up to the NCAA DII status.

Through all these changes, Dominey's teams reflected the same core values and principles embodied by previous teams: hard work, teamwork, relentless determination, a resilient heart, hustle, and discipline. James Dominey had an uncommon commitment to excellence that spanned 29 years as Head Coach at Valdosta State!

Willie Oxford, James Dominey and Tim Dominey

13

1971-72 Championships Keep Rolling

1971-72: The Rebels Championship Express Keeps Rolling!

Just a reminder that the test of any great organizational culture occurs when there is a change in leadership at the top. Which direction will the culture move afterward? Will it continue to ascend or crumble? The Rebels had two head coaches move on in the last four years, had maintained continuity and forward momentum after the change. With Jim Melvin's departure at the end of the 1971 season, Valdosta State quickly named James Dominey the fourth head coach of the Rebels, so the question regarding continuity was put to rest.

On the other hand, "Winnersville" had a year-round cauldron of percolating expectations. Dominey walked right into the furnace of those expectations, confident and competitive as ever! While the roar of Rebel Nation expectations never subsides, they were overshadowed by Coach Dominey's personal expectations and commitment to excellence every day—in every opportunity, much less game day! While the Rebel Tradition of winning the GIAC and playing for a trip to the National Championship would prove to be too much for some coaches and teams, not this coach nor his team. This team would be known for their intense defense, both full and half court, and consequently a more up tempo style of offense.

Under Coach Dominey, you had to be locked in and focused. He wanted to squeeze every ounce out of every opportunity! He continued to maintain and enhance the Rebel culture centered around teamwork, hard work, execution, relentless effort, and resilience. He was a competitor, which his teams reflected through their tenacity and aggressive defense. In fact, they played with a type of desperation on the defensive end of the floor, as well as on the boards. Simply, they continued the Rebel tradition of playing through the echo of the whistle.

Dominey's first year at the helm found a roster chocked full of returning lettermen and two incredible additions via recruiting: Ernest "Tiny" Hodge and Kenny Alston.

Returning were the following players:

- Willie Oxford, a junior, who had already broken the 1,000-point career threshold in his first two years, as well as being named to the GIAC All-Conference squad both years.
- Tim Dominey, a junior, who averaged 13.3 ppg last year.
- Eric Mance, a 6-4 sophomore wing, who was fully recovered from knee surgery that sidelined him last season.
- Roger Fleetwood, a 6-2 junior, who is the epitome of the 6th man that literally changes the energy on the floor when he checks in; not to mention his ability to handle the ball and shoot.
- Donnie Wisenbaker, a 5-10 sophomore, who would serve as the point guard for this squad.
- Jim Springfield, Tommy Pritchard, Jimmy Edwards, and Bob Donohoe would provide ample size and strength inside.
- Pete Lahey, a 6-1 senior, provided energy and relentless effort when he hit the floor.

Coach Dominey maintained the Rebels' Dawson connection (Willie Oxford) by landing a prized recruit, Kenny Alston, a 6-5 forward. Alston's competitive drive, augmented by his quickness and strength, enabled him to play 6-8. In addition, he had the offensive skills to score from anywhere on the floor. This was a freshman to watch as the year unfolded!

Tim Dominey, Donnie Wisenbaker, Willie Oxford, Kenny Alston and Ernest "Tiny" Hodge are introduced before a big game

Tiny Hodge came to Valdosta State from North Florida JC, just south of Valdosta in Madison. Although Tiny Hodge measured 6-8, his wingspan, quickness, vertical leap, and effort made it seem like he was 7 foot at times! With the addition of Hodge to the stockpiled interior talent, the Rebels were primed to be able to hit the glass with any team in the country.

The Rebels opened the season with victories over Armstrong State and Bethune Cookman, then lost three in a row: Florida Southern, FSU, and Oglethorpe. The regular season schedule was as tough as usual, providing opportunities from which to grow, and this team demonstrated their resilience, and ability to learn and adapt, as they rebounded by winning five in a row!

The Rebels were 3-0 in the GIAC as they entered the heart of the conference schedule in January. The schedule called for three-straight road games: West Georgia, LaGrange, and Armstrong State, which would begin to define the race for the championship and the Rebels' season.

West Georgia had hired former Georgia Tech All American Roger Kaiser the year before. Kaiser had been a successful high school coach in Atlanta prior to arriving at West Georgia. Kaiser's effect on the program was immediate; he brought in talented players such as Foots Walker and would become a serious challenger for the GIAC Championship. LaGrange College, under legendary Al Mariotti, would be a second challenger this year.

The Rebels got beat in Carroll-ton (92-82) and LaGrange (103-100), before they traveled to Savannah, where they were flat and lost 99-84. Tommy Johnson, Grad Assistant, tells what happened afterward that changed the direction of the season. "We got home around 4 a.m. Before we got off the bus, Coach Dominey told everyone to go put on their practice gear, we were going to go to work. We finished and left the gym around nine later that morning." The Rebels went on a four-game winning streak, before facing Georgia Southern in Statesboro, losing 93-83.

Tiny Hodge scores!

At this point in the conference season, the Rebels found themselves needing some help and knowing they had to close out the conference schedule with nothing but wins. The Rebels went on a roll, beating

Piedmont before facing West Georgia and LaGrange in Valdosta. The crowd for those games made the environment vocal and hostile, making it a harrowing environment for the visitors with dreams of a championship floating in their minds. The Rebel fanatics were lunatics in their advocacy for their Rebels!

The Rebels thumped West Georgia, 88-76, and edged LaGrange, 75-73. Tim Dominey hit the game winner against the Panthers, one of his patented rainbows that splash into the net! Dominey had 20 points, Oxford and Hodge 16 each, Alston with 11, and Wisenbaker with eight. The game was won on the defensive end of the floor and on the boards, where the Wrecking Crew (Hodge, Springfield, and company) manhandled the Panthers. After the dust settled, there was a three-way tie for first place between Valdosta State, West Georgia, and LaGrange.

Oxford goes in for a score as Wisenbaker position for a pass

A game to determine the champion was held in Americus, a neutral site, between West Georgia and Valdosta State. The Rebels delivered their best performance of the season, rocking West Georgia, 122-84. The Rebels knocked down a school-record 57 field goals in this game. The Rebels won their 11th GIAC Championship in 12 years and made their sixth-straight trip to the District 25 Championship.

It was onto the District 25 Championship where the Rebels would line up against rival Albany State, featuring 7-footer Caldwell Jones. The gym was packed and rocking as the Rams rolled in, with everyone expecting an up and down the floor affair. Albany State Coach Rainey changed his strategy and made sure the Rams got the ball in deep to CJ, who scored 40 points in a hard-fought 80-78 victory over the Rebels. Coach Dominey to this day says the defeat at the hands of Albany State in the District final was one of the toughest losses to handle of his career.

The Rebels finished the season 18-8 overall and 10-2 in the GIAC.

The season saw several school records fall:

Jim Springfield scores against West Georgia

- Most points scored in a game: 122 vs. West Georgia. (Record has since been broken.)
- Most field goals in a game: 57 vs. West Georgia.
- Highest points per game average: 89.
- Highest rebound average per game: 59.
- Most times scoring 100+ points: seven games.
- Most Free Throws Attempted in a Season: Willie Oxford's 190. At this point in his career, Oxford had made 366 FTs.

The team had five players average double figures: Tim Dominey, Willie Oxford, Kenny Alston, Tiny Hodge, and Eric Mance. Clearly, the

Rebels' offensive success was developed around having two All-GIAC guards in Dominey and Oxford, but more importantly a team who was unselfish and willing to get the next guy a better shot. Although the Rebels ran and ran often, it was based on their dominance of the boards by Hodge and his Wrecking Crew!

Willie Oxford scored a total of 1,491 points in his three-year career, which placed him seventh on the all-time points scored list at the time. By the time he graduated, Willie scored 1,914 points, placing him second on the list. Tim Dominey in two years had scored 803 points and by the time he completed his eligibility would have 1,193 points (10th place on the all-time points scored list). This dynamic duo opened the floor up for everyone else and both were just as willing to share the ball as score with it!

It is impossible to discuss the recipe for success for this team without pointing out the work of the Wrecking Crew on the glass. Tiny Hodge, Kenny Alston, Eric Mance, Jimmy Edwards, Jim Springfield, and Bob Donahoe stormed the boards night after night, often with abandon! Coach Dominey preaches that defense and rebounding come down to courage, determination and desire, and basketball IQ (knowing where to go to get the best shot at the carom). Tiny Hodge was slender by any measure, but his heart and guts are immeasurable, which rubbed off on everyone else in the Wrecking Crew.

Roger Fleetwood finished his career as a Rebel with three-straight GIAC titles, after transferring from Indiana State. Roger was a co-captain for the Rebels and exemplified the Rebel Spirit in every way, on and off the court. His spirit is unmatched, and it infected everyone in the locker room and on the floor. Floor leadership was in great hands with Fleetwood. He could handle the ball, play great on ball and help-side defense, and was always ready to take a tough shot in tough circumstances. Roger upheld the great tradition of 6th men who wore the Rebel jersey, inspiring those around to play through the echo of the whistle! James Dominey's first season ended with a GIAC Championship, a slew of school records set, and a heart-breaking loss to Albany State in the District Championship. Coach Dominey successfully introduced himself to the head coaching fraternity and world as the coach who would consistently win championships, recruit talented players that align with the Rebel Spirit on and off the court, and develop (empower and equip) the team to find a way to win against adversity because of his uncommon commitment to excellence!

Wisenbaker scores as Alstons follows

EPILOGUE: The Legacies and Leadership Lessons from the Valdosta State Basketball Dynasty

This book project began with a simple objective: Document the history of the Rebel basketball teams (1954-1972) for us and our families. As we began this journey, we found that although our memories are somewhat faded, many moments associated with this chapter of our lives were burned indelibly in our hearts and minds! These memorable moments are what we sought to present through the stories, scores, and records surrounding each of the respective seasons, as well as the reasons why the Rebels were dominant during this era.

As we interviewed former coaches, players, and staff, as well as reviewed their letters describing their years as a Rebel, the consensus was that we passionately believe that athletics is one of the finest preparations for most of the intricacies, adversities, and darknesses life can throw at you. The lessons we learned while playing basketball for the Rebels have proven to be priceless, both professionally and personally. As we bring this project and book to a close, we want to share with you the life lessons and legacies that we uncovered within the wins, losses, and championships.

A clear legacy was the tradition of winning 11 conference championships in 12 years between 1960-1972. Mike Perry explains the Colson legacy in this regard, writing "tradition cannot be bought; it must be earned. The

	GIAC Champions	District 25 Champions	NAIA Sweet 16
	• 1960-61	• 1966-67	• 1966-67
	• 1961-62	• 1967-68	• 1967-68
	• 1962-63	• 1968-69	
	• 1963-64		
	• 1965-86		
	• 1966-67		
	• 1967-68		
	• 1968-69		
	• 1969-70		
	• 1970-71		
	• 1971-72		

process usually takes several years to take root, and if done correctly, will carry on for years. From 1961-1968, under Coach Colson's leadership, the Valdosta State Rebels developed that Championship Tradition and culture," which continued under Melvin and Dominey. Not until we began researching information and data for this project did we conclude that the Rebel teams of this era were in fact a dynasty within the GIAC. No other collegiate program in Georgia accomplished this level of dominance and a tradition of excellence within their respective conference.

As players and as a team, we remained in the moment, embracing the game within the context of the season, and focusing on the moment at hand. While those who played, coached, and served were aware of the accomplishments at the time, never once did we consider the breadth and scope of those accomplishments within the context of historical significance. It was a great life lesson for every one of us—stay in the NOW, which is critical to any consistent success.

Bench Leadership Legacies and Leadership Lessons

An overwhelming sentiment among former players and staff was that one of the major contributing factors to our accomplishments was the "overall depth and quality of the coaching tree" in this era! Championship cultures begin with the Head Coach or CEO or President. Valdosta State basketball had an extraordinary pedigree of transformational leadership talent and skill in this era (and throughout the 20th century) due to decisions made by Walter Cottingham, Gary Colson, Jim Melvin, and James Dominey.

Jim Nichols said "Looking back now and viewing the string of GIAC Championships, with every other conference team trying to knock us off, is quite an accomplishment. That Colson, Melvin, and Dominey were able to take an assortment of talent and mold it into championship teams—says a lot about their leadership talent and skills."

1. All four knew what they were looking for in talent and culture fit in their assistant and staff; following Jim Collins' counsel in *Built to Last*, "Get the right people on the bus, get them in the right seat, and great things can happen!" Walter Cottingham saw something in Gary Colson as a high school senior that he believed would make him a great leader, someone to build a young program around. Gary Colson saw leadership and energy in Jim Melvin, a JC transfer, that he believed could provide direction and influence on the floor for his young Rebels. Jim Melvin saw a leadership style, skills, and coaching acumen in James Dominey that would not only complement his leadership style but could one day stand at the helm of the Valdosta State program!

2. The coaches were men of integrity, genuine, and authentic; being clear what they stood for and then walked the talk. Consequently, the players followed based on their actions rather than the magnitude of their declarations. Bill Long said that Coach Cottingham was as great an example of a man of integrity as there was. Ray McCully shared that "Coach Colson kept the commitments he made to me." Another example of the integrity of the coaches was that numerous players returned to school after their eligibility expired and their scholarships were honored until they graduated.

3. All three of these coaches were extreme competitors, whether it was on the tennis, badminton, or basketball court. They were bringing max effort and intensity, and you had better be prepared or you would get blown away. If there is one trait that was identical in the three of them, this is it! This translated into the energy and passion they presented concepts at practice, as well

as the manner in which they demonstrated how they wanted the skill executed. In short, they would "get after you in a New York minute!"

4. They were excellent evaluators of talent and character, refusing to allow noise from the outside to distract or prevent them from making the best decision for the team. Each coach knew precisely what he wanted from each position on the floor; the traits, character, and skill set needed. They sought players who could fit into and adapt (were coachable) to the Rebel culture and systems. If you get the right people on the bus, in the right seats, set the proper expectations, facilitate their learning, development, and understanding, then great things happen!

5. One of the salient characteristics of transformational leaders is the inspirational effect they have on their constituents, in this case their players, the administration, student body, and the community. The opening lines of Walt Whitman's "O Captain! My Captain!" captures the inspirational power this type of transformational leadership has: **"O Captain! my Captain! our fearful trip is done, the ship has weather'd every rack, the prize we sought is won."** Although Whitman was referencing Abraham Lincoln and his leadership during the Civil War, the analogy solidly reflects the adversity the Rebel leaders and teams faced from year to year, the coaches always discovering strategies to capitalize on the talent, while infusing the team with confidence and belief in doing the impossible! Jim Melvin said he purposefully tried to inspire people to reach for the improbable, to reach beyond "what is" for "what can be," explaining, "One of the great things I love most about leadership is teaching a person how to reach higher and higher, to achieve great things with his or her talent!" Jim Springfield said, "Coach Melvin's aspirational leadership had an incredible effect on my life and career. I felt like he brought out the best in me and everyone." Doug Parrish shared that his time under Colson "ignited my desire to conquer all challenges that confronted me in life."

6. Although each coach had different approaches to how they deal with players, different views of offense and defense, and different ways to prepare, all of their teams had a clear identity, vision, and most importantly, a clear sense of the coach's expectations. Colson, Melvin, and Dominey believed that "winners act like winners before they're winners, and champions behave like champions before they're champions" by setting and sharing clear goals, as well as the high expectations of themselves and the team. They believed that "players thrive in an environment where they know exactly what is expected of them—even when those expectations are very high."

7. The coaches developed a Learning Culture that required everyone to understand that Mastery is a never ending process, not some destination at which you eventually arrive. Although we chased perfection, we were taught we would experience periods of excellence along the journey. What could be learned from defeat was fervently consumed to make us better as players and as a team. Mastering one's craft requires an extraordinary level of humility, as well as a high level of self-awareness where ego and assumptions are set aside in favor of lifelong learning.

   a. The coaches established a culture of accountability, in which they were accountable, as well as the players and staff. Accountability worked in the Rebel culture because the coaches were willing to admit mistakes, which makes them unique in that many head coaches prefer to finger point and cover up errors in judgment. All the coaches were adamant that everyone buy into the Rebel culture, regardless of talent. Marty Lehmann recalled that Coach Melvin pulled a starter during a game because of his refusal to play team basketball; the player cleaned his locker out that night and went home. Consequently, the coach's actions created high levels of respect and trust within the team.

b. Trust among the team members is critical to developing a championship culture, and the ultimate prerequisite is for the team to develop an inherent trust among themselves and with the coaches and staff. Mike Perry noted that "learning to trust others to do their job was a critical lesson the offensive system taught me. The learning process helped me understand that while everyone had limitations, the offensive system (and team) overcame those limitations, allowing everyone to focus on their strengths. The lesson of trusting others to do their job was applied in my career and company!" Angie Devivo added "we had a role and a job to do, some were scorers, some rebounders, and some defenders, etc. We were committed to fulfilling our role and responsibilities to the team, no matter what!"

c. The coaches understood the importance of including praise, constructive feedback, and encouragement. Jim Melvin said "praise is one of the most effective tools at a leader's disposal. Few things offer greater return on less investment than praise. 'I believe in you' are four powerful words!" Gerald Davidson shared the impact of Colson taking a few moments to send him a Christmas card "acknowledging how effectively I had defended the top scorer in the last game before the break" and how effective his incentive program (hamburger steaks for drawing a charge) were. A number of players pointed out how each of the coaches encouraged them to participate in student life, as well as reaching out to the students and community to encourage their support of the program as fans and boosters. As Jim Nichols points out, "the Rebels developed a great deal of support, as fans and boosters, from the community" thanks to the tireless efforts of the coaches.

d. Each coach built their culture around intense practices that required hard work (max effort), ongoing learning and instruction (focus), and extremely competitive drills to shape and develop the championship culture and team camaraderie. The coaches used competition to ensure each player faced tough challenges every day, thereby earning their position and playing time. Ray McCully added that Colson "recruited some exceptional players, made sure there was competition for playing time, that we were well prepared and instilled in us the belief we could compete with anyone!" Practices were structured not only for competition sake, but for learning and applying knowledge on the floor, to enhance skill development, avoid mental mistakes, play through the echo of the whistle, finish, learn how to fight through fatigue, and, most of all, learning how to do what is best for the team. Repeatedly heard from former players was that Colson, Melvin, and Dominey were all incredible teachers, intensely focused on getting the fundamentals done correctly, offering explanations and examples to ensure the players understood the concept and executed it within their drill. Gerald Davidson added, "Gary Colson was a great teacher who believed in hard work and teamwork. He taught us how to run the Wheel and we ran it to perfection, cutting other teams to ribbons." Tim Dominey shared practice "was where we learned what the principle of going the extra mile means literally and figuratively playing through the echo of the whistle. I use it with my colleagues today, I refer to it as GEM—Going the Extra Mile!"

e. A vital part of the team-building process under the head coaches was how they used the furnace of practice time to shape and develop a Shared Vision and enhance the camaraderie and chemistry between players. The Rebel tradition included the expectation that experienced players would participate in the education and development of the new players. It was through this legacy that the coaches moved the team from "me to us," expecting everyone to look beyond their self-interest, thereby effectively creating that unique Shared Vision; as well as stir their players to reach their potential as individuals and as a unit! Marty Lehmann described the help and insights Seniors Ron Fortner, Bob Lamphier, and Bryan Phillips provided his freshman year, when he was converted from a post player to playing the wing: "The older players would help you learn the system, which was part of the Valdosta State culture. In fact, they would bend over backwards to help you." Roger Fleetwood adds, "The time under both Coach Melvin and Coach Dominey helped solidify my belief that it was critical to not put yourself first. In a team, everyone needs to be selfless. When each man gives their best selflessly, it gives the team the best chance to win. When everyone embraces that belief, I learned how much of a difference it can make in the team chemistry and performance."

f. A critical piece of the learning culture created by the coaches, and a by-product of players helping other players learn the traditions and systems, was the creation of a sense of family. The coaches walked that talk—they made sure our needs were met, sometimes in creative fashion like complimentary haircuts from "Barbershop Bob" or meals from the "Boarding House" or rooms in the "Shack." Consequently, we knew they cared about us! Tim Dominey shared that he learned the importance of helping others get what they want, setting aside personal agendas and objectives, which has carried over into his career. Specifically, how necessary it is to develop an uncommon level of trust within an organization, so you pull for one another rather than against one another. Another player shared how Coach Colson helped him work through a bout of homesickness that would have otherwise cost him academically and athletically. What impressed this player was how "Coach met me where I was at, spoke to me with genuine care and concern, and then went to bat for me with the school."

g. With the coaches demonstrating respect, empathy, actively listening, and providing constructive feedback, it was a model of behavior players imitated. Ben Bates recalls the slogan was "one for all and all for one!" Bryan Phillips mentioned that there was never a pecking order. "Whether you were a player or a manager or trainer or cheerleader, you were considered a part of the Rebel family." In other words, there were no barriers such as rank or title to clog up healthy and productive team chemistry. Tommy Johnson takes it a step further, explaining "the Rebel teams of this era were a brotherhood, not just a group of basketball players." A common refrain from former players is that when they went to Valdosta State, they had no idea they would have lifetime relationships; relationships that never disappear off the radar screen in life, since one of the key principles of Rebel Tradition was to place the needs of others above your own—be there to help! It is not by accident the Rebel teams performed at high levels, at times beyond their potential ceiling, they felt (and still feel) as if they are part of something special—"a family that treats them right."

h. In addition, each coach was obsessed with preparation and details, planning for as many contingencies as they could conceive. If we heard the following once, we heard it hundreds of times: "When you prepare for everything, you are ready for anything." The coaches were never trying to fool anyone with their style or schemes, rather they obsessed over fundamentals, believing their players play faster, smarter, and make fewer mistakes than the players they face. Consequently, "the team developed an elevated level of confidence; going into every game thoroughly prepared, full of belief and courage, confident we would prevail." For example, Colson sent McCully a detailed study of the Wheel months before he arrived as a Freshman, knowing McCully would digest the offense and arrive ready to run it.

i. The head coaches understood what it took to develop a championship culture that included the ability to adapt, adjust and overcome adversity and challenges. Being aware of the talent on the roster and schedule, the coaches constantly adjusted and adapted the offensive and defensive systems and strategies. Melvin and Dominey tweaked the Wheel when they took the helm and added "Dominey D" along with a full-court press to the stable of strategic actions. Players were expected to know and apply the fundamentals, as well as make the necessary adjustments from one game plan to the next. One edge of Valdosta State's was the level of strategic adjustments the coaches constantly made. "We learned that we would be forced by circumstances and challenges to adapt and adjust if we wanted to overcome the next opponent, which it turns out is very similar to life, stay out of the ruts—they're just long coffins." Consequently, we learned that knowledge is dynamic, it changes from moment to moment, situation to situation, and game to game. The thirst for knowledge and ensuing Mastery was unquenchable!

Colson never stopped growing. Mike Perry pointed out "Gary Colson was instrumental in making the 3-point shot a reality in college basketball," and was constantly adapting throughout his career. Fred Gibbons shared that "Colson's original yearly Coaching Peer Group (George Raveling, Sonny Smith, Bill Foster, and Ralph Miller, to name a few of the coaches who attended) became a much copied strategy for coaches who wanted to continue to grow the game and grow their knowledge of the game. I took the same strategy into my professional career as an Executive Coach, setting up Peer Groups of leaders from across industries and regions to encourage and empower executive leaders with opportunities to stretch and grow." In addition, Gibbons said "when Coach Melvin left to earn his Ed.D. in Educational Leadership, it challenged and encouraged me to look at life beyond the game and gym."

Lastly, Bill Walsh in his book, *The Score Takes Care of Itself*, makes the point that the highest form of leadership occurs when leaders produce more leaders. In coaching circles, it is commonplace to check out a coach's tree of coaching prodigies. For example, Nick Saban's coaching tree is substantial at this point; ADs want to hire someone who has worked within Saban's program. The larger and more critical question regarding a respective coach's leadership impact is *where and what became of the players and staff who played and worked for the coach? To what extent were they able and willing to take the lessons learned under Coaches Cottingham, Colson, Colson, or Dominey, and apply them to their life and career?*

The list of accomplished leaders from this era spans successful leaders in education, medical research, business, the military, ministry, agriculture, etc. Tommy Johnson says "we took on the personality and style of our leaders (Colson in basketball and Grant in baseball), and there's no price tag you can put on this experience. They showed us how to prepare, compete to win championships, then succeed in life and relationships." "The proof is in the pudding" and these men went into the world after graduation and positively affected the people they interacted with, managed, and led, as well as developing organizations that were and are world class. In this picture, Colson is surrounded by a group that would become leaders in their respective professional endeavors!

Although the personalities and leadership styles of the four coaches are different, their core beliefs and values, vision, competitiveness, knowledge of the game, and commitment to excellence were aligned, enabling continuity and consistency from one season to the next season, as well as from one coach to the next coach. The Rebel culture never wavered or waffled through the winds of change and adversity. The sails were adjusted and the captain at the helm led the team to the next championship on the horizon—the Due North of the Rebel culture! The Rebels captured the proverbial "lightning in a bottle" during these years; because each coach nurtured this culture, and it was built to last!

These leaders were not gods, simply real men who taught us how to be greater men! They would be first to say that much of their success is rooted in the good fortune (fate smiling on the Rebels) to coach players with great talent and greater character at a great school in a rare community!

Floor Leadership (Captains and others) Legacies and Leadership Lessons

When the ball is tipped to begin a game, the coaches have pretty much done all they can, and the outcome rests on what the Floor Leaders (players) do from that point forward. Sam Walker noted that his research indicated "the most crucial ingredient in a team that achieves and sustains historic greatness is the character of the player(s) who lead it." Coach John Wooden stated that he believed that "winning takes some talent while repeating takes character." The Rebels' Floor Leadership (captains, as well as other players) over these 16 years were the glue and the driving force, the sparkplug, motivator, and disciplinarian within the locker room and on the floor that enabled the Rebels to remain elite in spite of changing coaches three times.

As we explored our memories, we could see the Floor Leaders play at levels that amazed their fans and tormented their opponents, elevating the energy on the floor and in the locker room to astronomical heights. These Rebel teams played and conducted themselves with character that was the embodiment of an uncommon spirit, the Rebel Spirit—playing through the echo of the whistle!

While the Rebel Spirit was tangibly recognized every year with an award voted by the players, the Rebel Spirit itself was seen daily within the locker room and practice, and on campus as Rebel leaders constantly motivated others with their passionate and extraordinary non-verbal actions. Tom Waits said, "The way you do anything is the way you do everything" and players all the way through to the managers exuded this character trait. These men would "go the extra mile" which included diving for loose balls, setting picks, rebounding like their very next breath depended on it, being there to help on defense, etc. While just one Rebel won the coveted Rebel Spirit Award every season, there could have been a couple of others just as easy. Following are the elements that make up the most valued commodity on championship teams, the Rebel Spirit.

First and foremost, while the roster was made up of talented players, more importantly they were unselfish, and team oriented up and down the bench. Although the Rebels had their share of All Conference, All District, and All Americans, they were as unselfish and team oriented as the rest of the squad. What set the Rebels apart personnel-wise was the depth of the bench where you found the players who, although they were not starting, were as integral to the heart and soul of the team as the starters. From the point guards to the wings to the inside players to the 6th men, the players from this era demonstrated a high level of commitment to team over self, choosing rather to display their powerful will to win, fiery competitiveness, and passionate desire.

It is safe to say, "if you wore a game shirt for the Rebels, you had the Rebel Spirit and were committed to making a difference when you went on the floor!" More often than not, this commitment to playing like a zealot is what made the difference in many Rebel victories, since when other teams substituted for starters, their bench players could not match the level of energy and intensity of those coming off of the Rebel bench.

Second, the Rebels were doggedly disciplined, determined, relentless, and resilient. Simply stated, they were Rebel Tough. This type of toughness does not have anything to do with physicality or athleticism; it is an attitude, an intangible skill that has to be developed over time according to Jay Bilas, former Duke All-American and ESPN analyst. Bilas describes this toughness as the ability to bend but not break and bounce back. Mike Krzyzewski says, "when you get knocked down, it's mental toughness that always gets you back up, not physical toughness." Tom Izzo shares that "toughness is being willing to do what it takes to make a difference; refusing to accept ceilings or limitations, striving for that next gear." US Soccer midfielder Julie Foudy shares that "toughness is your willingness to fight through whatever comes in your way. It is how you deal with adversity and what you learn from the others you are invested with." Colson, Melvin, and Dominey actively recruited players with this type of character, players, and staff who relentlessly pursued perfection and were resilient, refusing to give in to adversity, whose "get back up" quotient was about 110%. We were coached to look past the obstacles, to focus solely on the opportunities!

The Rebels had this in spades, from the starting five throughout the bench and staff. This characteristic (and the fact that players who came off the bench played with this toughness) is another thread that separated the Rebels from other teams in this era. Gordon Guinn has told his Rebel friends over the years that the reason he and his Shorter teammates could not conquer the Rebels was that the Rebels were just "tougher." Marty Lehmann swears that the practice sessions under Colson, Melvin, and Dominey "made us tougher, smarter, and more disciplined than our opponents." Ritch will tell anyone within earshot that Ben Bates defended him tougher than any opponent, every day! Roger Fleetwood shared that the battles he had defending John Trimnell at practice helped develop his toughness, skills, and confidence.

Third, Rebel leaders were humble, willing to do the thankless jobs in the shadows on both the floor and in the locker room. During the interviews and research, we heard how former teammates had helped other teammates over the years, whether it was a phone call or card or assistance in some form. Tommy Johnson referred to this era as a "brotherhood," a band of relationships that never disappear off your radar, where any of us would stop what we are doing to listen to and help another teammate. That was the way we played, though—be there to help your teammate whether that meant set a screen or help side defense. We believed that our "actions spoke louder than words" and being there to help is how respect and commitment are displayed in the locker room and on the floor. While practice, which determined playing time, was extremely competitive, the level of respect for one another was evident in the unity of the teams from year to year. Numerous players shared that when they arrived on campus, they were not humble, but learned that lesson from the coaches and older players. It changed their perspective on themselves, others, and life.

Fourth, while Rebel leaders were typically low key, they played through the echo of the whistle. Gerald Davidson and Steve Doughty were both short in stature but played defense with a level of intensity that made them affect other team's star players like they were 6-4. Likewise, John Trimnell was 6-2, but played with a ferocity on defense and on the boards that made him appear to be 6-7. Fred Gibbons recalled, "Berry's leading scorer coming off the floor at halftime in Rome begging Trimnell to stop hitting and bumping him." Bryan Phillips remembered his game-long tussle with Dave Cowens in Tallahassee, saying, "I was confident they were going to let us play and they did. I made sure Cowens knew I was there and made every foul worth the cost."

Lastly, Rebel leaders were able to maintain ironclad emotional control while in the midst of the furnace of intense, championship competition. The discipline ingrained in the Rebel tradition expected players, bench, and staff to maintain emotional control during these crucible-like moments in high leverage games. The Rebels' ability to win conference championship after conference championship is a testament to their character, especially remaining under control, more than their talent.

The Architects of the Rebels Success, the head coaches, clearly knew how to select not only talented players, but more importantly, young men with great character. Young men who were willing to be coached, embraced teamwork and hard work, and were most of all, relentless and resilient—Rebel Tough!

Consequently, the Valdosta State Rebels of this era represent the gold standard in athletics, 11 GIAC Championships in 12 years! A dynasty unlike any other in the history of college basketball in Georgia!

Bibliography

- *Built to Last* (1994) and *Good to Great* (2001) by Jim Collins.
- *Emotional Intelligence* by Daniel Goleman, 1995.
- *Getting to Us* by Seth Davis, 2018.
- *Leaders Eat Last* by Simon Sinek, 2014.
- *Leadership* by James MacGregor Burns, 1978.
- *Leadership & Performance Beyond Expectations* by Bernard Bass, 1985.
- *My Losing Season* by Pat Conroy, 2003.
- *Resonant Leadership* by Richard Boyatzis and Annie McKee, 2005.
- *The Captain Class* by Sam Walker, 2017.
- *The Fifth Discipline* by Peter Senge, 1990.
- *The Score Takes Care of Itself* (2010) & *Finding the Winning Edge* (1997) by Bill Walsh.
- *Toughness* by Jay Bilas, 2013.
- *Valdosta Daily Times* articles from 1958-1972.
- *Valdosta State Pinecone* from 1954-72.

Acknowledgements

One of the late Wake Forest coach Skip Prosser's favorite maxims was, "Never delay gratitude." I am extremely grateful to so many for their guidance, inspiration, and help throughout this research and writing project, as well as in my life. I was positively influenced by so many people, that in writing this book, I was able to better appreciate just how fortunate I have been to have these great people in my life. Each has made me better in a multitude of ways and helped to make me a more effective leader.

I was a teammate to some extraordinary men, none closer to me than John Trimnell, Marty Lehmann, and Roger Fleetwood. These teammates left an indelible impression on my heart and mind regarding what toughness is, both in word and deed. They were especially instrumental in helping me understand and define the qualities displayed by our teammates through the most challenging times of our years together at Valdosta State. They have been and will always be brothers.

In the course of this project, I was blessed to get to know the earlier Rebels of the era under review—especially the Rebel Legacy Project Team made up of Tommy Johnson, Ray McCully, Jim Nichols, Mike Perry, and Bobby Ritch. Their tireless energy and enthusiasm in contacting former players was a great example of "playing through the echo of the whistle." Their memories and insights into the earlier seasons made all the difference to the accuracy and vivid accounts of the games. More than this project, I can see why the Rebels were a dynasty. All of us lived and breathed team first, and were relentless and resilient in our pursuit of perfection. Tommy Johnson accurately describes the players of this era as a "brotherhood!"

As a manager and trainer, then grad assistant, I was incredibly blessed to serve under Gary Colson, Jim Melvin, and James Dominey. All three acted as coach, mentor, confidant and, most important, my friend throughout my life. Their insights and time were invaluable in this research and writing project. I count my decision to enroll at Valdosta State at the invitation of Coach Melvin, and then to move to Malibu with Gary Colson, as the second most important and meaningful decisions in my life. The lessons these coaches taught me, sometimes against my will, shaped the way I lived my life.

Over my years in athletics, ministry, and as an executive coach, I have been fortunate to get to know national leaders like "Big" Don Williams, Ken Blanchard, Dr. Paul Faulkner, Dr. Carl Mitchell, Mrs. M. Norvel Young, and Dr. Carol Pearson, and to call them my friend, as well as mentor and coach. They were there to provide critical feedback and insights at pivotal junctures in my life. Lynn Cain, former USC Trojan and Atlanta Falcon, is an incredible person and was an amazing athlete and, more importantly, is my best friend in life; from whom I have learned so much about what real resilience and toughness is. Through these people, I learned the role and importance that leadership and hope plays in life, as well as in athletics.

In researching and assembling this book, I strove to draw upon the values, principles, and lessons I learned and observed from people I have studied and worked with over the years. I cannot thank these people enough: Bob Fraley, Bob Thomas, Charlie and Amy Jo Runnels, Mike Phipps, T.W. Harvey, Kermit Southard, Tim and Ann Lewis, Wally and Charlotte Wilkerson, David Kelly, Bill and Carol Hale, Charles and Joann Warlick, Bill and Laura Long, Larry and Pat Kraxberger, and Phil and Donna Waldron.

Next up, my deepest appreciation to my son and daughter in law, Jonathan and Laura Gibbons, who provided their professional skills, staff, and resources to create the cover design, artwork, and initial formatting. These skills and resources proved to be invaluable.

Closing out projects, as well as championship games, requires skill and tenacity. Writing a book means finding a publisher that is capable, as well as interested in the project. As we began this phase of the project Jim Springfield (who joined the Rebels as a freshman in 1970, my last year) volunteered to serve as the publisher, offering to print the book through his publishing company. This is the same attitude Jim displayed on the court as a teammate and fraternity brother, always willing to jump in and do what was necessary to win. His actions further exemplify the Rebel Spirit.

I now understand how and why editors are so valuable to writers. It is a painstaking task, often without any glamour or glitz. I have been blessed with some great editors beginning with my wife, Leslie, followed by a great team of friends from Mike Perry to Ray McCully to Mike Chason (Chason Enterprises, LLC) to Dante Skourellos, Esq. They attacked this project like editing ninjas, for which I'm grateful.

In addition, Ray McCully worked with John Crawford, Vice President for *University* Advancement and Chief Executive Officer of the *VSU* Foundation, Inc., to make the book available through the VSU Alumni Relations Office. Consequently the book project became a reality because of the unselfish efforts of all of the friends and teammates, to them I offer my sincerest gratitude and appreciation!

There is another group of people I need to acknowledge for great inspiration in the writing of this book—the physical therapists who served me during my rehabilitation after contracting polio in the fall of 1953. These men and women taught me literally how to get back up on my own after falling down and try to take the next step. They taught me how to set goals, walking with the help of a rail, then moving on to the next challenge—walking 10 feet without any assistance. Then 30 feet, across the room, then down the hall. At 5 years old, I understood what overcoming adversity was all about, and what resilient and relentless effort was. A second inspiration was PGA Professional Wiley Watkins, who taught me how to swing a golf club after I left rehab and encouraged me to continue to "find a way" to lower my golf handicap without the benefit of the large muscle groups in the lower body. A third inspiration were my grandparents, John and Sadie Lance from Webster, FL, who taught me the core values and beliefs I hold to this day. And last, my stepfather, Bud Bossong, who took me to the football coach at Wilson Junior HS in Tampa and asked the coach if he needed a manager, which was the entry point into a great brotherhood of athletics for me.

Last, but not least, is my wife, Leslie, and my two boys, Joshua and Jonathan. The biggest honor of my life is to be called their Dad. The decision to date and marry Leslie was the most important decision I made in my life. Since the first semester at Pepperdine, where I met Leslie, I have had my best friend next to me. Together, we have walked through life facing and overcoming adversity, and climbing mountains that at times seemed improbable, although finally reaching the pinnacle more times than I can count. Leslie is one of the most compassionate yet toughest people I know, able to corral 25-30 elementary children every day in her career as an educator; then doing home visits to ensure their parents understood their child's assignments. Her gift for editing and revising got me through graduate school, as well as this project. Her new title is Editor and Chief, without whose candid feedback would have meant my tendency to be verbose would have been more exposed. Proverbs 31 describes her to a "T."

I remain, still playing through the echo of the whistle!

Fred Gibbons

www.ingramcontent.com/pod-product-compliance
Lightning Source LLC
Chambersburg PA
CBHW071857090426
42811CB00004B/645